Succeed on the Standardized Test

This Book Includes:

- 2 Summative Assessments (SA)
- Additional practice questions
- Detailed answer explanations for every question
- EBSR (Evidence Based Selected Response) questions
  TECR (Technology Enhanced Constructed Response) questions
  PCRs (Prose Constructed Response(s)) questions
- Strategies for building speed and accuracy
- Content aligned with the Common Core State Standards

Plus access to Online Workbooks which include:

- Hundreds of practice questions
- Self-paced learning and personalized score reports
- Instant feedback after completion of the workbook

Complement Classroom Learning All Year

Using the Lumos Study Program, parents and teachers can reinforce the classroom learning experience for children. It creates a collaborative learning platform for students, teachers and parents.

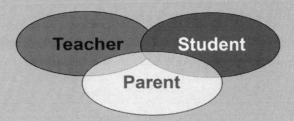

Used in Schools and Public Libraries
To Improve Student Achievement

Lumos Learning

Common Core Assessments and Online Workbooks: Grade 7 Language Arts and Literacy, PARCC Edition

Contributing Editor   - **Suzanne Riordan**
Contributing Editor   - **Eric Ibsen-Johnson**
Contributing Editor   - **George Smith**
Curriculum Director   - **Marisa Adams**
Executive Producer   - **Mukunda Krishnaswamy**
Designer and Illustrator - **Sowmya R.**

ISBN-10: 1940484162

ISBN-13: 978-1-940484-16-7

Printed in the United States of America

For permissions and additional information contact us

Lumos Information Services, LLC
PO Box 1575, Piscataway, NJ 08855-1575
http://www.LumosLearning.com

Email: support@lumoslearning.com
Tel: (732) 384-0146
Fax: (866) 283-6471

Lumos Learning

Table of Contents

Introduction

The Common Core State Standards Initiative (CCSS) was created from the need to have more robust and rigorous guidelines, which could be standardized from state to state. These guidelines create a learning environment where students will be able to graduate high school with all skills necessary to be active and successful members of society, whether they take a role in the workforce or in some sort of post-secondary education.

Once the CCSS were fully developed and implemented, it became necessary to devise a way to ensure they were assessed appropriately. To this end, states adopting the CCSS have joined one of two consortia, either PARCC or Smarter Balanced.

What is PARCC?

The Partnership for Assessment of Readiness and College and Careers (PARCC) is one of the two state consortiums responsible for developing assessments aligned to the new, more rigorous Common Core State Standards. A combination of educational leaders from PARCC Governing and Participating states, along with test developers, have worked together to create the new computer based English Language Arts and Math Assessments.

PARCC's first round of testing occurred during the 2014-2015 school year. As they remain committed to doing what is best for students, and listening to the parents, educators, and students in the consortium, PARCC worked on a redesign of their test for the following years. They decreased testing time and the amount of tests students would need to take beginning in the 2015-2016 school year.

How Can the Lumos Study Program Prepare Students for PARCC Tests?

At Lumos Learning, we believe that year-long learning and adequate practice before the actual test are the keys to success on these standardized tests. We have designed the Lumos study program to help students get plenty of realistic practice before the test and to promote year-long collaborative learning.

This is a Lumos **tedBook**™. It connects you to Online Workbooks and additional resources using

a number of devices including Android phones, iPhones, tablets and personal computers. The Lumos StepUp Online Workbooks are designed to promote year-long learning. It is a simple program students can securely access using a computer or device with internet access. It consists of hundreds of grade appropriate questions, aligned to the new Common Core State Standards. Students will get instant feedback and can review their answers anytime. Each student's answers and progress can be reviewed by parents and educators to reinforce the learning experience.

How to use this book effectively

The Lumos Program is a flexible learning tool. It can be adapted to suit a student's skill level and the time available to practice before standardized tests. Here are some tips to help you use this book and the online workbooks effectively:

Students

- Take one Summative Assessment (SA).
- Use the "Related Lumos StepUp® Online Workbook" in the Answer Key section to identify the topic that is related to each question.
- Use the Online workbooks to practice your areas of difficulty and complement classroom learning.
- Download the Lumos StepUp® app using the instructions provided in "How can I Download the App" to have anywhere access to online resources.
- Have open-ended questions evaluated by a teacher or parent, keeping in mind the scoring rubrics.
- Review additional questions in the practice area of the book.
- Take the second Summative Assessment as you get close to the test date.
- Complete the test in a quiet place, following the test guidelines. Practice tests provide you an opportunity to improve your test taking skills and to review topics included in the PARCC test.

Parents

- Familiarize yourself with the PARCC test format and expectations.
- Get useful information about your school by downloading the Lumos SchoolUp™ app. Please follow directions provided in "How to download Lumos SchoolUp™ App" section of this chapter.
- Help your child use Lumos StepUp® Online Workbooks by following the instructions in "How to access the Lumos Online Workbooks" section of this chapter.
- Help your child download the Lumos StepUp® app using the instructions provided in "How can I Download the App" section of this chapter.
- Review your child's performance in the "Lumos Online Workbooks" periodically. You can do this by simply asking your child to log into the system online and selecting the subject area you wish to review.
- Review your child's work in the practice Summative Assessments and Practice Section.

LumosLearning.com

Teachers

- You can use the Lumos online programs along with this book to complement and extend your classroom instruction.

- Get a Free Teacher account by visiting LumosLearning.com/a/stepupbasic

  This Lumos StepUp® Basic account will help you:

  - Create up to 30 student accounts.
  - Review the online work of your students.
  - Easily access CCSS.
  - Create and share information about your classroom or school events.
  - Get insights into students' strengths and weakness in specific content areas.

  NOTE: There is a limit of one grade and subject per teacher for the free account.

- Download the Lumos SchoolUp™ mobile app using the instructions provided in "How can I download the App" section of this chapter.

PARCC Frequently Asked Questions

What Will PARCC English Language Assessments Look Like?

In many ways, the PARCC assessments will be unlike anything many students have ever seen. The tests will be conducted online, requiring students complete tasks to assess a deeper understanding of the CCSS. The students will be assessed once 75% of the year has been completed in one Summative based assessment and the Summative Assessment will be broken into three units: Unit 1, Unit 2, and Unit 3.

The test will consist of a combination of three new types of questions:

EBSR (Evidence Based Selected Response) – students will need to use evidence to prove their answer, choices will be often be given.

TECR (Technology Enhanced Constructed Response) – students will use technology to show comprehension. For example, they may be asked to drag and drop, cut and paste, or highlight their responses.

PCRs (Prose Constructed Response(s)) – students will be required to construct written response to a test prompt using specific evidence and details from the passages they have read.

The time for each ELA unit is described below:

Estimated Time on Task in Minutes			
Grade	Unit 1	Unit 2	Unit 3
3	90	75	90
4	90	90	90
5	90	90	90
6	110	110	90
7	110	110	90
8	110	110	90

What is a PARCC Aligned Test Practice Book?

Inside this book, you will find two full-length practice tests that are similar to the PARCC tests students will take to assess their mastery of CCSS aligned curriculum. Completing these tests will help students master the different areas that are included in newly aligned standardized tests and practice test taking skills. The results will help the students and educators get insights into students' strengths and weaknesses in specific content areas. These insights could be used to help students strengthen their skills in difficult topics and to improve speed and accuracy while taking the test.

LumosLearning.com

In addition, this book also contains a Practice Section with passages and questions broken into the key categories students will see in the three Summative Units: Literary text, Research Simulation (Informational text), and Narrative Writing.

How is this Lumos tedBook aligned to PARCC Guidelines?

Although the PARCC assessments will be conducted online, the practice tests here have been created to accurately reflect the depth and rigor of PARCC tasks in a pencil and paper format. Students will still be exposed to the TECR technology style questions so they become familiar with the wording and how to think through these types of tasks.

This edition of the practice test book was created in the FALL 2015 and aligned to the most current PARCC standards released to date. Some changes will occur as PARCC continues to release new information in the spring of 2016 and beyond.

How to access the Lumos Online Workbooks

First Time Access:

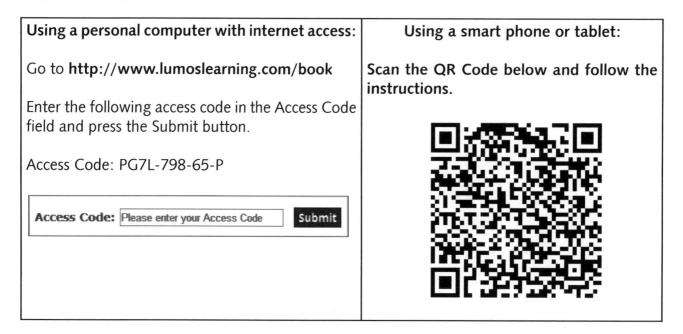

Using a personal computer with internet access:

Go to **http://www.lumoslearning.com/book**

Enter the following access code in the Access Code field and press the Submit button.

Access Code: PG7L-798-65-P

Access Code: Please enter your Access Code Submit

Using a smart phone or tablet:

Scan the QR Code below and follow the instructions.

In the next screen, click on the "New User" button to register your user name and password.

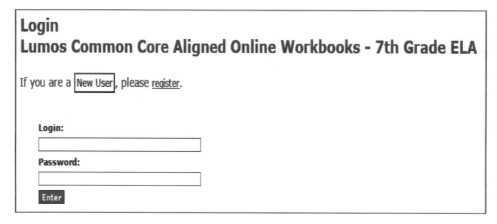

Login
Lumos Common Core Aligned Online Workbooks - 7th Grade ELA

If you are a New User, please register.

Login:

Password:

Enter

Subsequent Access:

After you establish your user id and password for subsequent access, simply login with your account information.

What if I buy more than one Lumos Study Program?

Please note that you can use all Online Workbooks with one User ID and Password. If you buy more than one book, you will access them with the same account.

Go back to the **http://www.lumoslearning.com/book** link and enter the access code provided in the second book. In the next screen simply login using your previously created account.

Lumos StepUp® Mobile App FAQ For Students

What is the Lumos StepUp® App?

It is a FREE application you can download onto your Android smart phones, tablets, iPhones, and iPads.

What are the Benefits of the StepUp® App?

This mobile application gives convenient access to Practice Tests, Common Core State Standards, Online Workbooks, and learning resources through your smart phone and tablet computers.

- Eleven Technology enhanced question types in both MATH and ELA
- Sample questions for Arithmetic drills
- Standard specific sample questions
- Instant access to the Common Core State Standards
- Jokes and cartoons to make learning fun!

Do I Need the StepUp® App to Access Online Workbooks?

No, you can access Lumos StepUp® Online Workbooks through a personal computer. The StepUp® app simply enhances your learning experience and allows you to conveniently access StepUp® Online Workbooks and additional resources through your smart phone or tablet.

How can I Download the App?

Visit **lumoslearning.com/a/stepup-app** using your smart phone or tablet and follow the instructions to download the app.

QR Code
for Smart Phone
Or Tablet Users

Lumos SchoolUp™ Mobile App FAQ For Parents and Teachers

What is the Lumos SchoolUp™ App?

It is a FREE App that helps parents and teachers get a wide range of useful information about their school. It can be downloaded onto smartphones and tablets from popular App Stores.

What are the Benefits of the Lumos SchoolUp™ App?

It provides convenient access to
- School "Stickies". A Sticky could be information about an upcoming test, homework, extra curricular activities and other school events. Parents and educators can easily create their own sticky and share with the school community.
- Common Core State Standards.
- Educational blogs.
- StepUp™ student activity reports.

How can I Download the App?

Visit **lumoslearning.com/a/schoolup-app** using your smartphone or tablet and follow the instructions provided to download the App. Alternatively, scan the QR Code provided below using your smartphone or tablet computer.

**QR Code
for Smart Phone
Or Tablet Users**

Test Taking Tips

1) **The day before the test, make sure you get a good night's sleep.**

2) **On the day of the test, be sure to eat a good hearty breakfast! Also, be sure to arrive at school on time.**

3) **During the test:**

- **Read every question carefully.**

  - Do not spend too much time on any one question. Work steadily through all questions in the section.
  - Attempt all of the questions even if you are not sure of some answers.
  - If you run into a difficult question, eliminate as many choices as you can and then pick the best one from the remaining choices. Intelligent guessing will help you increase your score.
  - Also, mark the question so that if you have extra time, you can return to it after you reach the end of the section. Try to erase the marks after you complete the work.
  - Some questions may refer to a graph, chart, or other kind of picture. Carefully review the graphic before answering the question.
  - Be sure to include explanations for your written responses and show all work.

- **While Answering Multiple-Choice (EBSR) questions.**

  - Completely fill in the bubble corresponding to your answer choice.
  - Read all of the answer choices, even if think you have found the correct answer.

- **While Answering TECR questions.**

  - Read the directions of each question. Some might ask you to drag something, others to select, and still others to highlight. Follow all instructions of the question (or questions if it is in multiple parts)

Prose Constructed Response(PCR) Rubric

Each Summative Assessment includes different writing tasks which will be scored by hand. In order to effectively assess students' writing, a standardized rubric will be use. The following rubric will be used throughout this workbook as a means of assessing the writing prompts. Students should be familiar with the rubric as it is an excellent guide to the type of responses they should be creating. The Detailed Answer section of each Summative Assessment will include the page number of the rubric so students can see the scoring guide.

Literary & Informational Rubric

4 Point Score	3 Point Score	2 Point Score	1 Point Score	0 Point Score
The student response fully and thoughtfully addresses all parts of the prompt.	The student response addresses all parts of the prompt.	The student response addresses basic parts of the prompt.	The student response addresses limited parts of the prompt.	The student response addresses no parts of the prompt.
The student response demonstrates a full and thorough understanding of what it is written explicitly in the text.	The student response demonstrates an effective understanding of what it is written explicitly in the text.	The student response demonstrates some understanding of what it is written explicitly in the text.	The student response demonstrates a minimal understanding of most of the concepts written explicitly in the text.	The student response demonstrates little or no understanding of most of the concepts written explicitly in the text.
The student response demonstrates a full and thorough analysis of the text by making accurate and meaningful inferences from the text.	The student response demonstrates a mostly thorough analysis of the text by making accurate and meaningful inferences from the text.	The student response demonstrates some analysis of the text by making accurate reasonable inferences from the text.	The student response demonstrates an attempt at analysis of the text by making inferences that are supported, in part, by the text.	The student response makes little or no attempt at analysis of the text by making inferences, or inferences or not reasonable and not supported by the text.
The student response is completely and intentionally supported by explicit references from the text.	The student response is completely and intentionally supported by explicit references from the text.	The student response is somewhat supported by intentional, explicit references from the text.	The student response is supported by limited, general or vague references from the text.	The student response is supported is not intentionally supported by references from the text.
The student response is effectively organized, clear, and has an effective style.	The student response is mostly organized, clear, and has a mostly effective style.	The student response has some organization and is somewhat clear with a somewhat effective style.	The student response has limited organization and clarity and is written in a minimally effective style.	The student response has no organization, is not clear, and/or has no, or an inappropriate, style.

LumosLearning.com

Narrative Rubric

4 Point Score	3 Point Score	2 Point Score	1 Point Score	0 Point Score
The student response is developed effectively, has narrative elements, and remains consistent to the task.	The student response is developed mostly effectively, has most narrative elements, and remains mostly consistent to the task.	The student response is developed somewhat effective, has general narrative elements, and remains somewhat consistent to the task.	The student response is developed minimally, has limited narrative elements and limited consistency to the task.	The student response is not developed and is inappropriate to the task.
The student response is effectively organized, clear, and has an effective style.	The student response is mostly organized, clear, and has a mostly effective style.	The student response has some organization and is somewhat clear with a somewhat effective style.	The student response has limited organization and clarity and is written in a minimally effective style.	The student response has no organization, is not clear, and/or has no, or an inappropriate, style.
The student response shows full understanding and application of conventions of the English. There may be some minor errors in grammar, mechanics, and word usage. The mean is effective and clear.	The student response shows full understanding and application of the conventions of English. There may be a few minor errors in grammar, mechanics, and word usage. The mean is effective and clear.	The student response shows some understanding and application of the conventions of English. There may be minor errors in grammar, mechanics, and word usage. The meaning is somewhat effective and generally clear.	The student response shows limited understanding and application of the conventions of English. There may be some minor errors in grammar, mechanics, and word usage. The mean is generally clear.	The student response shows no real understanding and application of the conventions of English. There may be frequent and varied errors in grammar, mechanics, and word usage. The mean is ineffective and unclear.

Summative Assessment (SA) - 1

Student Name:
Test Date:

Start Time:
End Time:

Here are some reminders for when you are taking the Grade 7 ELA Summative Assessment (SA)

- You may look back at the reading passage as often as you want.
- Read each question carefully and think about the answer. Then completely fill in the circle next to your choice.
- If you do not know the answer to a question, go on to the next question and come back to the skipped question later.

Unit 1

The Little Thief
By Horace E. Scudder

(1)   IN one of the beautiful cities of Italy there stood a tall marble column, and on the top of the column was a statue of bronze, which shone in the sun. It was a statue of Justice, and Justice held in one hand a pair of scales; that was to say that every deed would be weighed in the balances: and in the other hand Justice held a sword; that was to say that when a man was weighed in the balances and found wanting, Justice was ready with a sword to put him to death.

(2)   Now for many years this statue stood for the government of the city. Justice was done to everyone. The law was observed by the rulers, who were fair in their dealings with men, and upright. But in the course of time the rulers became evil. They no longer governed justly, and the poor did not feel that they were treated by the law as the rich were treated, and this story is meant to show it.

(3)   In one of the palaces of the city there was a poor maid-servant whom we will call Martha. She went in and out about her duty, and was a faithful little thing. Although there were many jewels and pieces of money in her lady's chamber, she never took anything, and no one thought her any other than a good, honest girl.

(4)   But one day, when she came to help her lady dress for a great ball, she could not find a pearl necklace. It had been laid on the table, her lady said, and now it was not there. Martha looked everywhere, but could not find it. It was a warm night, the window was open, and she looked out. She did not think the necklace could have been blown out, but she had looked everywhere else.

              LumosLearning.com   ▲

(5) No, there was no sign of it. It had not fallen upon the stone ledge below the window. Not far away was the bronze figure of Justice, and in the darkness there was a curious sight. She could not see the stone pillar, but the bronze figure stood out against the sky as if it were flying through the air. This curious sight kept her looking, and made her forget for a moment what had happened.

(6) "Martha!" called her lady sharply, and Martha drew her head in and turned red as she thought of what she had been doing. Her lady looked at her keenly.

(7) "Martha," said she, suddenly, "you took the necklace. You are a little thief!"

(8) Martha was frightened at these words. She had never been called by such a name before, and she was confused, and knew not what to say. So she looked down and said nothing. The lady was angry.

(9) "I know you are a thief!" she said again, "a little thief!"

(10) "I am not," cried Martha, but the lady had made up her mind to it, and, as the necklace could not be found, she was certain Martha had taken it.

(11) Poor Martha! She had no friends now, and she could not prove she had not taken the necklace. She could only say she had not. To be sure, it was not in her little box, nor in any dress she had, nor anywhere in the little room where she slept. They only said she must have been very cunning to hide it away so carefully.

(12) And now Martha was put in prison, and the evil judges were more afraid of displeasing the great lady of the palace than of doing an unjust deed. They tried Martha, they found her guilty, and they condemned her to be put to death.

(13) It was a strange comment on the great bronze figure of Justice that the gallows on which Martha was to be hanged should be placed just under the figure, at the foot of the column. Yet so it was, and the day came for Martha to be hanged. The cruel judges gave her no hope.

(14) The day came, and it was dark and lowering. It was almost as if the heavens frowned on the city. The people gathered and Martha mounted the platform on which the gallows stood. Low mutterings were heard. The skies grew black. There was a sudden blinding light and a great crash. A bolt of lightning had plunged down. For a moment the people were stunned. Poor Martha thought she had been struck.

(15) But she had not been struck. The lightning, however, had come so near that it had struck the arm of Justice that held the scales, and down had come the scales to the ground. The scales fell, indeed, at Martha's feet, and when she could see, oh joy! there lay the gleaming necklace of pearls! It was twined in the clay of a nest!

(16) The secret was out. A magpie had stolen the necklace from the table in the palace, had flown with it out of the window to the nest he was building in the scales in the hand of Justice. Perhaps he was working it into the nest at the very moment when Martha was looking at the bronze figure.

(17) At any rate, justice was done at last to little Martha, though men had been unjust.

1. **PART A**

   From the passage above, what does the word <u>cunning</u> mean as it is used in paragraph 11?

   Ⓐ Crafty and devious
   Ⓑ Manipulative and strange
   Ⓒ Caring and smart
   Ⓓ Bold and aggressive

   PART B

   What evidence from the passage above best supports your answer in part A? Write the letter of your choice in the box below.

   Ⓐ For a moment the people were stunned.
   Ⓑ She could only say she had not.
   Ⓒ To be sure, it was not in her little box.
   Ⓓ To hide it away so carefully.

2. **After reading the cause in the box labeled CAUSE, pick the correct letter that is the effect and write it in the box labelled EFFECT.**

   CAUSE   **EFFECT**

   | Lightning hit the bronze statue | → | |

        LumosLearning.com   ▲

POSSIBLE EFFECTS

Ⓐ Martha was proven innocent.
Ⓑ The town caught on fire.
Ⓒ Everyone was surprised to see the bird fall.
Ⓓ The wealthy lady was proven to be the thief.

3.   What is the overall theme of the story?

Ⓐ Justice will never be served when the wealthy are involved.
Ⓑ Justice will eventually be served.
Ⓒ Justice is blind and always balanced.
Ⓓ Justice is broken at times.

Read the poem and answer the questions that follow.

Justice
By Ella Wheeler Wilcox

However inexplicable may seem
Event and circumstance upon this earth,
Though favours fall on those whom none esteem,
And insult and indifference greet worth;
Though poverty repays the life of toil,
And riches spring where idle feet have trod,
And storms lay waste the patiently tilled soil -
Yet Justice sways the universe of God.

As undisturbed the stately stars remain
Beyond the glare of day's obscuring light,
So Justice dwells, though mortal eyes in vain
Seek it persistently by reason's sight.
But when, once freed, the illumined soul looks out.
Its cry will be, 'O God, how could I doubt!'

4. **What does the word <u>illumined</u> mean in Stanza 2?**

Ⓐ **Bright and cheery**
Ⓑ **Irreverent**
Ⓒ **Enlightened**
Ⓓ **Unintelligent**

5. **Select the phrase from the poem that best indicates the author's purpose for using the word illumined.**

Ⓐ **So Justice dwells, though mortal eyes in vain**
Ⓑ **Though poverty repays the life of toil,**
Ⓒ **Its cry will be, 'O God, how could I doubt!'**
Ⓓ **As undisturbed the stately stars remain**

LumosLearning.com ▲

6. In the box below, write the letters of the descriptions of unjust moments in the poem above. You may use more than one phrase.

Ⓐ Though favours fall on those whom none esteem,
Ⓑ Beyond the glare of day's obscuring light
Ⓒ So Justice dwells, though mortal eyes in vain
Ⓓ And insult and indifference greet worth;
Ⓔ And riches spring where idle feet have trod,
Ⓕ And storms lay waste the patiently tilled soil

```



```

7. You have just read two stories with similar themes. Write a personal narrative describing a time when you witnessed justice occurring in your life.

```












```

LumosLearning.com

Read "Double Davids" and answer the questions that follow

Double Davids
Author Unknown, Adapted by Marisa Adams

(1)   "Hi David, I'm David."

(2)   Those four words started what was, quite possibly, the weirdest conversation ever. I had been minding my own business, watching T.V. in the den, when the lights flickered and then went completely black along with all of the electricity, including the TV show I was watching. A moment later one, solitary lamp came back on, casting an eerie glow towards the middle of the room where a man was standing who looked vaguely like my Uncle Norman.

(3)   "Hi David, I'm David," he repeated.

(4)   Silence spanned the distance between us as my eyes darted to the cell phone beside me. I thought that if I could reach it, I could call 911. My parents had taught me plenty of times what to do in an emergency. For a split second, I even thought maybe I could jump out the half-open window, although it opened onto the roof on the second story.

(5)   "I know your parents taught you to call 911 in an emergency," said the guy. "And I know that you're wondering if you can reach your cell phone in time."

(6)   My heart started pounding in my chest and I was becoming terrified. Obviously this guy had been stalking me.

(7)   "I wouldn't recommend jumping out the half-open window either," he continued with a peculiar little smile. "It opens onto the roof on the second story."

(8)   Instantly my eyes widened as I realized I had just been thinking about that "H-how are you doing this?" I stammered. "Are you reading my mind?"

(9)   The Uncle Norman look alike simply scoffed and shook his head. "Not really. Well, sort of."

(10)   "What does that mean?"

(11)   "I'm reading my own mind," he said.

(12)   Nervously, I shifted on the couch as real fear started to course through my body. "I don't understand you! That doesn't make any sense!" Maybe if I told him that someone was coming home soon, he would get scared and leave.

(13) "There's no point telling me that someone will return home soon because we both know that's not true," he continued and I shivered again. "Relax," he said. "You're the absolute last person in the world I would hurt. That would be fatally ignorant."

(14) "Why me?" I stammered out, knowing my heartbeat was racing wildly.

(15) "Because if I hurt you, I hurt me," he said. Lifting an eyebrow, he sat in the chair next to my couch, watching me carefully the entire time. "I'll explain, but you'll have a hard time accepting it."

(16) I took a deep breath to tried and calm my nerves, thinking if I just listened to him, maybe he would go away and I would be safe. Quietly, I whispered, "I'll try."

(17) His lips curled into a deeper smile as he slapped his hands on his knees. "Wonderful! I knew you were a smart cookie! OK, I am David Sean Lamont."

(18) "That's my name!" I exclaimed, interrupting him mid-sentence.

(19) "Don't interrupt, me. It's rude and I know we were taught better than that." Nodding my head quickly in agreement, I exhaled another breath as he continued. "I was born January 11, 1992."

(20) "That's when I was born! You're trying to mess with me!"

(21) "I told you that you would have a hard time accepting my explanation. The fact is, I am you. An older you."

(22) "There's no way – "

(23) "Just hear me out and stop interrupting. Man, I was obnoxious when I was young!" Shaking his head, he continued "I was 16 years old, sitting in this room, watching T.V. A guy came from the future and told me that he was me, and that he had invented a time machine in the future. He explained he had come back to see himself; in fact, it was the exact same conversation you and I are having now."

(24) "Time machine?" I asked weakly.

(25) "Yes, a time machine. I'm you, David, and I've just come back in time."

(26) Looking around the room warily, I couldn't help but asking, "Did you really invent a time machine?" I was actually half starting to believe it.

LumosLearning.com   ▲

(27) "We did, I did. Or, rather, we will, since it will happen in December of the year 2040."

(28) "Where is this machine?" I could hear the excitement in his voice but I still wasn't quite sure I was ready to believe him.

(29) "It doesn't go back and forth in time, the person does."

(30) I could almost believe it. I didn't think it could just be a coincidence that he seemed to know everything I was thinking. But, I had to find a way to reassure myself. "If you really came from the future," I said, "tell me something about it, so I can test you. Tell me who will win all the baseball games in the major leagues tomorrow."

(31) "I can't remember that far back, and we never liked baseball that much. But more importantly, I can't tell you anything about the future. If I did, you would have knowledge you are not supposed to have, and that could mess with the time stream."

(32) I couldn't help but scoff at him; that wasn't any kind of real proof. "So why are you here?" I asked.

(33) "Just to say 'hello,' and look at me," he said. "Goodbye, David, take very good care of yourself."

(34) "But I – " I began to say, and then the lights dimmed again. When they came back on, he was gone. The T.V. came back on. It was an old movie, called "Back to the Future."

(35) That made me laugh nervously, but when the laughter passed, I had a brilliant idea. Immediately, I grabbed a pencil and a pad of paper and starting taking very close notes about the movie.

8. **What mood is established by the author's description of the setting in paragraph 2?**

   Ⓐ **Clinical and unemotional**
   Ⓑ **Exciting and adventurous**
   Ⓒ **Mysterious and frightening**
   Ⓓ **Celebratory and joyful**

9.   Which of the following would be the best subtitle for this story?

Ⓐ "A Visit from a Friend"
Ⓑ "When an Emergency Strikes"
Ⓒ "The Man Who Could Read Minds"
Ⓓ "Traveling through Time"

10.   Read the descriptions of differences between younger David and older David. Select the choice that most accurately reflects the difference and write it in the box.

Ⓐ Younger David is trustworthy while older David is happy.
Ⓑ Younger David is cautious while older David is confident.
Ⓒ Younger David is confident while older David scared
Ⓓ Younger David is excited while older David is more reserved.

```



```

11.   What type of figurative language is used in paragraph 17 of the story?

Ⓐ Metaphor
Ⓑ Simile
Ⓒ Alliteration
Ⓓ Onomatopoeia

Unit 2

Read "How to Succeed as an Inventor: Chapter 1 and answer the questions that follow.

How to Succeed as an Inventor: Chapter 1
by Goodwin B. Smith

"Patience and the investment of time and labor for future results are essential factors in every inventor's success."

(1)   The field of invention is closed to no one. The studious mechanic may design and improve on the machine he operates. The day laborer, if dissatisfied with his lot, may devise means for lessening the toil of his class, and largely increase his earning capacity. The busy housewife, not content with the drudgery incident to her household cares, may devise a means or article which will lighten her task, and prove a blessing to her sisters. The plodding clerk, without an iota of mechanical knowledge, may perfect a system or an office appliance which will prove of vast benefit to himself and his fellows. The scientist may discover new forces and make new applications of old principles which will make the world marvel,—and so on through the whole category of crafts, occupations and professions.

(2)   If one of the old Kings of Israel, centuries ago, voiced the sentiment that there was nothing new under the sun, do we not possess, at the present time, a similar mental attitude, and are we not apt to say with him that there appears to be "nothing new under the sun"? Civilization begets new needs and wants; opportunities for new invention are multiplying at a tremendous rate. In other words, where an inventor, two centuries ago, would have had one hundred chances to "make good," today the chances are multiplied many thousand-fold.

(3)   No avenue of business can open up the possibilities of such enormous honors and fabulous money returns as a real invention which is in universal demand. The discoveries of the past form a record which is not only glorious, but points the man of genius of today in an unswerving manner to the possibilities which the future holds, and which are vastly greater than anything which has gone before. Each age finds the people convinced that human ingenuity has reached the summit of achievement, but the future will find forces, mechanical principles and combinations which will excite wonder, and prove to be of incalculable benefit to mankind.

(4)   Our old friend Darius Green and his flying machine, that we heard about when we were children, was not as great a fool as he was imputed to be. Witness at the present time the marvelous results attained by inventors with air ships. We are proud of Wilbur and Orville Wright, who at this writing have just broken all records for Aeroplanes, or "machines heavier than air." It seems that in five or ten years from now the navigation of the air will be a problem perfectly solved.

(5) (Since writing the above, on Thursday, September 17th, Orville Wright, at Fort Myer, Va., met with an accident to his machine, which resulted in the death of Lieutenant Selfridge, of the U.S. Army, and severe injuries to the inventor. The accident is said to have been due to the breaking of one of the propellers.)

(6) When you think that the first locomotives that were invented were considered wonders if they made a speed of eight to ten miles per hour, the chances are that within the next few years we will have airships going through space at incredible rates of speed.

(7) We might also, at this time, refer to the experiments of Count Zeppelin and Santos-Dumont, and the American, Professor Baldwin, in "dirigible balloons." This type of airships will undoubtedly be superseded by the "Aeroplane," or the "Helicopter." The principal inventors in this line are Henry Farman, the French inventor, and Delagrange, the German. Wright Brothers hold the world's record, at this time.

(8) Little did Murdock (who erected, in 1792, while an engineer in Cornwall, England, a little gasometer which produced gas enough to light his house and office) think that in the year 1908 no house would be considered as modern unless it was fully equipped with the gas for lighting and heating which he discovered and brought to practical use. It is also said that "while Murdock resided in Cornwall he made gas from every substance he could think of, and had bladders filled with it, with which, and his little steam carriage running on the road, he used to astonish the people." No one is astonished at "little steam carriages," or, in other words, automobiles, nowadays, one hundred and sixteen years later.

(9) Our grandparents, when they were young people, imagined that they were living in the "Golden Age," and yet we today would consider their lack of what we nowadays consider positive necessities a mighty primitive and inconvenient manner in which to live. When the "wisest man," centuries ago, is chronicled as saying, "There is nothing new under the sun," they lived in tents, rode camels, fought with bows and arrows, sling shots and battering rams! While the Tower of Babel was possibly the first "skyscraper," it did not contain express elevators, hot and cold water, telephones, call boxes, yale locks, granolithic floors, fire escapes, transom lifts, automatic sprinklers, stationary wash stands, water closets, steam or hot water heat, electric and gas lights, push buttons, sash weights, and so on ad infinitum. So you can readily appreciate the marvelous strides the human race is making in the way of material development, and all, or nearly all of which has been due to the fertile brain and nimble wit of the inventors! Who will have the temerity to say when and where this development will stop, when Solomon, centuries ago, thought they had reached the limit?

       ▲

(10) What will be the next wonderful invention? For instance, the perfected telephote? You, by stepping into a cabinet in Philadelphia, could have your photograph taken and shown in Boston, all by and through an electric wire! The Telephote may transmit light and color as the Telephone does sound; why not a combination of the two, so you can see your friend perfectly when you talk to him on the 'phone?

(11) Our grandparents thought they were as comfortable as possible, and they were, because they did not know any better. Do we know better? One hundred years from now, possibly, our great, great-grandchildren will consider us as having lived in the "stone age." The field of invention has no bars up,—you, all of us, are free to enter.

12. **PART A**

What is the meaning of the word <u>primitive</u> mentioned in paragraph 9?

Ⓐ **Not developed**
Ⓑ **Old fashioned**
Ⓒ **Modern**
Ⓓ **Necessary**

PART B

Which detail from the story best supports your answer in Part A?

Ⓐ **Our grandparents thought they were as comfortable as possible, and they were, because they did not know any better.**
Ⓑ **Who will have the temerity to say when and where this development will stop, when Solomon, centuries ago, thought they had reached the limit?**
Ⓒ **When the "wisest man," centuries ago, is chronicled as saying, "There is nothing new under the sun," they lived in tents, rode camels, fought with bows and arrows, sling shots and battering rams!**
Ⓓ **The field of invention has no bars up,—you, all of us, are free to enter.**

13. **According to the passage above, what is the primary reason new ideas and items are explored and invented?**

Ⓐ **to help women in the kitchen and around the home as they are completing their tasks**
Ⓑ **to ensure people who are learning to fly can do so safely**
Ⓒ **to move people from a primitive way of life to the "Golden Age"**
Ⓓ **to solve people's problems and explore new ways of doing things**

14. Select the letters of the words chosen to describe inventions? In the box below, write the letters of he three most important descriptors of inventions as mentioned in the passage.

(A) primitive
(B) excite wonder
(C) fabulous money returns
(D) inconvenient manner
(E) incalculable benefit

Read "The Story of Albert Einstein" and answer the questions that follow.

The Story of Albert Einstein
Author Unknown

(1) Without any indication he was destined for something great, Albert Einstein was born on March 14, 1879. In fact, his mother thought Albert was extremely unusual. At the age of two-and-a-half, Einstein still wasn't talking. When he finally did learn to speak, he uttered everything twice.

(2) Einstein did not know what to do with other children and his playmates called him "Brother Boring." Because of that, the youngster played by himself much of the time. He especially loved mechanical toys and looked for them everywhere he went. Looking once at his newborn sister, Maja, he is believed to have said, "Fine, but where are her wheels?" Einstein began learning to play the violin at the age of six because his mother believed it was important. He later became a gifted amateur violinist, maintaining this skill throughout his life.

(3) Unfortunately, that awkwardness extended to school as well. A headmaster at one of his early schools once told his father that Einstein's profession wouldn't matter because, "he'll never be successful at anything." But Einstein was not a bad pupil. He went to high school in Munich, Germany, where his family moved when he was fifteen months old, and earned good grades in almost every subject. He hated the strict school environment though, and often clashed with his teachers. At the age of 15, Einstein felt so stifled there that he left the school for good. He then took the entrance exams for college and although he failed some, his scores for Physics and Math were so good, they let him into the school.

(4) In 1900, at the age of 21, Albert Einstein was a college graduate and was employed. He worked as a teaching assistant and gave private lessons on the violin before finally getting a job as a technical expert in Bern's patent office. While he was supposed to be paying careful attention to other people's inventions, he was secretly developing many ideas of his own.

(5) One of his famous papers, published in 1905, was Einstein's special Theory of Relativity. This theory had to do with time and distance not being absolute. His theory explained that two perfectly accurate and synced clocks would not continue to show the same time if they came together again after a journey where one traveled at a faster speed than the other. From this theory followed the world's most famous formula which described the relationships between mass and energy:

$$E = mc2$$

(6) In 1915, he published his General Theory of Relativity, which provided a new idea of gravity. An eclipse of the sun in 1919 brought proof that his theory was accurate. Einstein had correctly calculated, in advance, the extent to which the light from fixed stars would be deflected through the sun's gravitational field. The newspapers proclaimed his work as a 'scientific revolution.'

(7) Einstein received the Nobel Prize for Physics in 1921. He was showered with honors and invitations from all over the world and applauded by the press.

15. **PART A**

What is the meaning of the word <u>**awkwardness**</u> as it is used in paragraph 3 in the passage above?

Ⓐ Unnecessarily unique
Ⓑ Difficult to deal with
Ⓒ Indescribable
Ⓓ Unusual genius

PART B

What detail from the story above best supports your answer?

Ⓐ Einstein did not know what to do with other children and his playmates called him "Brother Boring."
Ⓑ But Einstein was not a bad pupil. He went to high school in Munich, Germany, where his family moved when he was fifteen months old.
Ⓒ He especially loved mechanical toys and looked for them everywhere he went.
Ⓓ While he was supposed to be paying careful attention to other people's inventions, he was secretly developing many ideas of his own.

16. Why does the author consider Einstein's job at Bern's Patent Office important enough to mention?

Ⓐ The job is the first one he was able to successfully hold down.
Ⓑ His love of playing the violin became more important than that job.
Ⓒ He was able to work there because he did not have to interact with people.
Ⓓ The job became a source of inspiration for him.

17. Create a sequence of important events in the story by choosing details from the story and placing them in the correct boxes below.

Ⓐ Einstein received the Nobel Prize for Physics in 1921. He was showered with honors and invitations from all over the world and applauded by the press.
Ⓑ An eclipse of the sun brought proof that his theory was accurate.
Ⓒ His scores for Physics and Math were so good, they let him into the school.
Ⓓ One of his famous papers, was Einstein's special Theory of Relativity.

Event 1	Event 2	Event 3	Event 4

LumosLearning.com ▲

Read "Steve Jobs" and answer the questions that follow.

Steve Jobs
Author Unknown

(1) Odds are, you've heard of iPods, iPhones, and Apple computers. And you've probably seen films like "Toy Story" or "Finding Nemo." But you may not have heard of the man who is behind the scenes of all these ventures. His name is Steve Jobs, and he may be the single most influential person in American popular culture.

(2) Jobs was born in 1955. He was a fairly good student in high school, and was admitted to Reed College in 1971. However, his interests lay elsewhere. As a resident of Cupertino, California, Jobs lived near many of the most important computer companies in the world. These firms were growing as they brought the use of computers to almost every kind of business. Jobs attended lectures and business presentations, and got a job working at Atari, an early manufacturer of video games. After just one semester at Reed, Jobs dropped out and returned to Atari, where he met another young computer enthusiast, Steve Wozniak.

(3) In 1976, Jobs and Wozniak founded Apple Computers. Wozniak was a very good computer engineer, which Jobs was not. Jobs' role was to organize the business, to bring in new ideas, and to direct the creativity of the designers. The vision that Jobs and Wozniak shared was one that not too many people took seriously at the time: personal computers. Most people in the computer industry considered this a ludicrous idea. Why would someone want to buy a computer for home use? After all, computers were good for working with large numbers or sets of information, but they weren't easy to learn and they didn't seem to fit into the average person's lifestyle.

(4) Jobs saw things differently. He imagined a computer that would be easy or even fun to use. He knew it would have to have a certain enjoyable style as well as practical use in the home, or people wouldn't buy it.

(5) That kind of thinking inspired Apple's first big success – the Macintosh computer, which came out in 1984. It was the first computer that used a white screen instead of black with green text. It was also the first to use a point-and-click mouse and pull- down command menus. Before that, computer users had to remember long lists of commands they had to type in order to get the computer to perform even simple tasks.

(6) The Macintosh was hardly Jobs' only success. He spent some time away from Apple in the late 1980's and early 1990's. During this time he became the owner of Pixar Animation, a film studio that focused on computer-based graphics. Pixar had a string of hits, including "The Incredibles," "Monsters, Inc.," and "WALL-E."

(7)   Jobs returned to head Apple and modernized the Macintosh line to take advantage of the growing internet boom. In 2001, Apple introduced the iPod, a device to play MP3 audio files, usually songs. Other devices already existed to play MP3s, but the iPod was easier to use, and it fit well with Apple's online music store, iTunes.

(8)   Similarly, when Apple came out a few years later with the iPhone, it was hardly the first cell phone. It wasn't necessarily the best. But its catchy graphics and ease of use have made it the most popular cell phone.

(9)   This is a theme that has run through all of Jobs' work. He has a tremendous sense of what people want. Jobs isn't a particularly impressive computer programmer, or designer. Thousands of people know more than he does about how to make a cell phone or music machine work. He doesn't write or direct films – but he is heavily involved in choosing which films Pixar will make. He has the ability to understand what entertains an average person.

(10)   This is true in the Macintosh, which has evolved from its early roots to become a favorite consumer brand. It's also true in the development of the iPod. As his engineers showed Jobs their plans, he kept instructing them to make it simpler. He wanted any song to be no more than two clicks away. That insistence on making the devices fit to people, rather than the other way around, is one of the reasons why he was voted America's Most Powerful Businessman of 2007 by Fortune magazine.

18.   **PART A**

Read the following quote from paragraph B in the article above: "Most people in the computer industry considered this a ludicrous idea." Which of the following is a synonym for <u>ludicrous</u>?

ⓐ **Unworkable**
ⓑ **Fantastic**
ⓒ **Absurd**
ⓓ **Attractive**

PART B

What evidence from the passage above supports your answer in PART A?

ⓐ **Jobs saw things differently. He imagined a computer that would be easy or even fun to use.**
ⓑ **Why would someone want to buy a computer for home use?**
ⓒ **That kind of thinking inspired Apple's first big success – the Macintosh computer,**
ⓓ **But its catchy graphics and ease of use have made it the most popular cell phone.**

19. Based on the quotes below, which of these people would most likely have shared Steve Jobs' opinions of how important computers should be in our lives?

   Ⓐ Pablo Picasso, who said, "But they are useless. They can only give you answers."
   Ⓑ Andy Rooney, who said, "Computers make it easier to do a lot of things, but most of the things they make it easier to do don't need to be done."
   Ⓒ Thomas J. Watson, the founder of IBM, who is alleged to have said in 1943, "I think there is a world market for maybe five computers."
   Ⓓ Albert Einstein, who said, "Computers are incredibly fast, accurate, and stupid. Human beings are incredibly slow, inaccurate, and brilliant. Together they are powerful beyond imagination."

20. Read the list of statements describing both Albert Einstein and Steve Jobs. Select the statement for each person that best supports the quote "The field of invention is closed to no one," as mentioned in the first passage *How to Succeed as an Inventor: Chapter 1*. Write the letter of each statement in the correct box below.

   Ⓐ He returned to head Apple and modernized the Macintosh line to take advantage of the growing internet boom.
   Ⓑ He received the Nobel Prize for Physics in 1921. He was showered with honors and invitations from all over the world and applauded by the press.
   Ⓒ The Macintosh was hardly his only success. He spent some time away from Apple in the late 1980's and early 1990's.
   Ⓓ A headmaster at one of his early schools once told his father that his profession wouldn't matter because, "he'll never be successful at anything."
   Ⓔ That insistence on making the devices fit to people, rather than the other way around, is what made him successful.
   Ⓕ The newspapers proclaimed his work as a 'scientific revolution.'
   Ⓖ After just one semester at the University, he dropped out and returned to work.

Albert Einstein	Steve Jobs

21. At the beginning of Chapter 1 from *How to Succeed as an Inventor,* the following quote is mentioned. Read the quote, choose one of the inventors mentioned: Albert Einstein or Steve Jobs, then write a reflective essay describing how patience and investment impacted the inventor of your choice.

"Patience and the investment of time and labor for future results are essential factors in every inventor's success."

Read "Captain Molly Pitcher" and answer the questions that follow

CAPTAIN MOLLY PITCHER
By Lawton B. Evans

(1) THE British had left Philadelphia, and were in full retreat across Jersey on their way to New York. Washington was right behind them, the front ranks of the American Army fighting the rear ranks of the British. It was a long, running fight. At last they came to Monmouth, and there a battle was begun. General Charles Lee, in charge of the American forces, acted so badly that the issue of the fight was long in doubt.

(2) When Washington saw the disorder of the troops, he was angry, and rebuked General Lee so harshly that the officer turned as white as a sheet. He was afterwards tried by court-martial and dismissed.

(3) Then Washington took charge himself. Orders flew thick and fast. Aids scurried in every direction, putting cannon in position, and getting ready for the renewed attack which was sure to come. Soon the guns roared, the heat of battle became terrible, and smoke covered the entire field; the dust and dirt were blinding. The men were suffering for lack of water. It was then that Molly Pitcher, the wife of one of the gunners, called out, "Go on with the firing. I will fetch water from the spring."

(4) The men waved their hands to her; she ran down the hill, drew water in a canteen, and carried it back and forth to the soldiers. She passed from cannon to cannon, while the men drank and kept on with their deadly work.

(5) How many times she did this no one knew, but, as she was coming once with her supply of water, a shot from the enemy struck her husband in the breast, and he fell beside his smoking cannon. Molly ran to him, and knelt down by him; one look was enough to convince her that he was dead.

(6) As she sat there in speechless grief, with the dead man's head in her lap, an officer rode up, and said to some soldiers, "Take this cannon to the rear; there is now no one to serve it."

(7) When Molly heard this, she sprang to her feet, and cried out, "Stop! That cannon shall not leave this field for lack of someone to serve it. Since they have killed my poor husband, I will take his place, and avenge his death."

(8)   With that, she seized the rammer from the hands of her dead husband, sprang to the muzzle of the piece, rammed home the powder, and stepped back, saying, "Ready!" Then the cannon blazed again, carrying death and dismay to the ranks of the enemy.

(9)   Molly Pitcher stood at her post as long as the battle lasted. Black with smoke, covered with dirt and dust, blinded by the heat, she did the work of a man. She never flinched for a moment, nor did she stop until the order came to cease firing.

(10)   Then she sat down on the ground by the side of her poor dead husband, took his head again in her lap, and gave way to her tears and grief.

(11)   Washington had seen her with her cannon during the battle. He admired her courage and patriotism, and sent for her to come to headquarters. He told her what a splendid deed of heroism she had done, and conferred on her an officer's commission. After that, she wore an epaulet, and everybody called her "Captain Molly."

22.   **What is the primary theme of the passage "Captain Molly Pitcher"?**

        Ⓐ **Serving others is a noble cause.**
        Ⓑ **Taking the time to understand priorities like water is important.**
        Ⓒ **Staying calm under pressure helps you make strong decisions.**
        Ⓓ **Seeking fame and titles will help you in life.**

23.   **Most of the only quotations throughout the passage belong to Molly Pitcher. Explain how the author's choice to use that dialogue impacted the passage.**

        Ⓐ **It allowed the reader to understand what Molly Pitcher was trying to express.**
        Ⓑ **It allowed the reader to hear certain sounds and understand them.**
        Ⓒ **It allowed the reader to feel how difficult a battle can be.**
        Ⓓ **It allowed the reader to step into the shoes of Molly and hear her thoughts and feelings.**

24.   **PART A**

        What is the meaning of the word <u>rebuked</u> as it is used in paragraph 2?

        Ⓐ **Express some displeasure**
        Ⓑ **Express extreme happiness**
        Ⓒ **Express sharp disapproval**
        Ⓓ **Express vague dislike**

                     LumosLearning.com   ▲

PART B

What evidence from the passage supports your answer in PART A?

Ⓐ sat there in speechless grief
Ⓑ so harshly that the officer turned as white as a sheet.
Ⓒ so badly that the issue of the fight was long in doubt.
Ⓓ nor did she stop until the order came to cease firing

25. Select the three phrases from below that best explain how Molly Pitcher came to be known as Captain Molly Pitcher. Write the letters of the three phrases into the box.

Ⓐ She sprang to her feet, and cried out, "Stop! That cannon shall not leave this field for lack of someone to serve it. Since they have killed my poor husband, I will take his place, and avenge his death."
Ⓑ The men were suffering for lack of water. It was then that Molly Pitcher, the wife of one of the gunners, called out, "Go on with the firing. I will fetch water from the spring."
Ⓒ An officer rode up, and said to some soldiers, "Take this cannon to the rear; there is now no one to serve it."
Ⓓ Then she sat down on the ground by the side of her poor dead husband, took his head again in her lap, and gave way to her tears and grief.
Ⓔ Molly Pitcher stood at her post as long as the battle lasted. Black with smoke, covered with dirt and dust, blinded by the heat, she did the work of a man.

26. PART A

How do Molly's actions in serving water to the soldiers impact their ability to fight?

Ⓐ The men had to stop and drink the water, causing them to lose precious time.
Ⓑ The soldiers were able to stay hydrated, allowing them to keep fighting.
Ⓒ The water became a distraction for the soldiers because there was not enough.
Ⓓ The water caused the soldiers to become sick and unable to fight.

PART B

What evidence from the passage above supports your answer in **PART A**?

Ⓐ The men were suffering for lack of water.

Ⓑ Soon the guns roared, the heat of battle became terrible, and smoke covered the entire field; the dust and dirt were blinding.

Ⓒ How many times she did this no one knew, but, as she was coming once with her supply of water, a shot rang out.

Ⓓ She passed from cannon to cannon, while the men drank and kept on with their deadly work.

    LumosLearning.com   ▲

Unit 3

Read the poem and answer the questions that follow.

The Rainy Day
By Henry Wadsworth Longfellow

(1)   The day is cold, and dark, and dreary;
        It rains, and the wind is never weary;
        The vine still clings to the mouldering* wall,
        But at every gust the dead leaves fall,

(2)   And the day is dark and dreary.
        My life is cold, and dark, and dreary;
        It rains, and the wind is never weary;
        My thoughts still cling to the mouldering Past,
        But the hopes of youth fall thick in the blast,

(3)   And the days are dark and dreary.
        Be still, sad heart! And cease repining;
        Behind the clouds is the sun still shining;
        Thy fate is the common fate of all,
        Into each life some rain must fall,

(4)   Some days must be dark and dreary.

* mouldering — decaying, fading

27.   What does <u>repining</u> mean in Stanza 3?

        Ⓐ Worrying
        Ⓑ Caring
        Ⓒ Thinking
        Ⓓ Living

28.   What is the overall theme of this poem?

        Ⓐ The world is a dreary place.
        Ⓑ The weather is unpredictable but occasionally the sun will shine.
        Ⓒ Life can be difficult at times, but there is always room for hope.
        Ⓓ Wind and dreary weather can make things difficult but you can have sunshine to help.

29. **What is the primary difference between Stanza 1 of the poem and Stanzas 2 and 3?**

    Ⓐ The first stanza discusses the weather and the other stanzas reflect on life.
    Ⓑ The first stanza primarily discusses the dismal weather and the later stanzas reflect on the brighter future.
    Ⓒ The first stanza focuses on young age and the later stanzas reflect on older age.
    Ⓓ Each stanza reflects on a different season.

30. **Poets often use imagery in their poems. Select the letters from the phrases on the left and place them in the correct "Imagery" boxes.**

    Ⓐ
    Ⓑ The wind is never weary
    Ⓒ But the hopes of youth fall thick in the blast
    Ⓓ Behind the clouds is the sun still shining
    Ⓔ And the days are dark and dreary
    My thoughts still cling to the mouldering Past

DESPAIR	HOPE	REPINING

31. **PART A**

    Who is the author addressing throughout the entire poem?

    Ⓐ The world around him.
    Ⓑ The readers of the poem.
    Ⓒ Himself
    Ⓓ His past

    PART B

    What evidence from the poem best supports your answer in part A?

    Ⓐ the hopes of youth
    Ⓑ the day is cold
    Ⓒ into each life
    Ⓓ my thoughts

LumosLearning.com

32. Longfellow uses this poem to talk about the dark times we must all go through at some point in our lives. Write a personal narrative about a difficult time you faced and include the moment you realized there was some light, some hope, in the situation.

Read the passage and answer the questions that follow.

The Secret of Everyday Things
SNOW
by Jean Henri Fabre

(1) "SNOW has the same origin as rain: it comes from vapor in the atmosphere, especially from vapor rising from the surface of the sea. When a sudden cooling-off takes place in clouds at a high elevation, the condensation of vapor is immediately followed by freezing, which turns water into ice.

(2) "I have already told you that cirrus clouds, which are the highest of all clouds and hence more exposed to cold than the others, are composed of extremely fine needles of ice. Lower clouds, too, if subjected to a sufficient degree of cold, undergo the same transformation. Then there follows a symmetrical grouping of adjacent needles in delicate six-pointed stars which, in greater or less numbers and heaped together at random, make a snowflake. Soon afterward, when it has grown too heavy to float in the air, the flake falls to the ground.

(3) "Examine attentively one that has just fallen on the dark background of your sleeve or cap. You will see a mass of beautiful little starry crystals so graceful in form, so delicate in structure, that the most skillful fingers could never hope to make anything like them. These exquisite formations, which put to shame our poor human artistry, have nevertheless sprung from the haphazard mingling of cloud-masses.

(4) "Such then is the nature of snow, the schoolboy's favorite plaything. From a somber and silent sky it falls softly, almost perpendicularly. The eye follows it in its fall. Above, in the gray depths, it looks like the confused whirling of a swarm of white insects; below it resembles a shower of down, each flake turning round and round and reaching the ground only after considerable hesitation. If the snowfall continues thus for a little while, everything will be hidden under a sheet of dazzling whiteness.

(5) "Now is the time for dusting the back of a schoolmate with a well-directed snowball, which will bring a prompt reply. Now is the time for rolling up an immense snowball which, turning over and over and creaking as it grows, at last becomes too large to move even under our united efforts. On top of this ball a similar one will be hoisted, then another still smaller on that, and the whole will be shaped into a grotesque giant having for mustache two large turkey feathers and for arms an old broomstick. But look out for the hands in modeling this masterpiece!

LumosLearning.com

More than one young sculptor will hasten to thrust them, aching with cold, into his pockets. But, though inactive himself, he will none the less give the others plenty of advice on how to finish off the colossus.

(6)   "Oh, how glorious is a holiday when there is snow on the ground! If I were to let myself go, how eloquent I could be on the subject! But, after all, what could I say that would be new to you? You know better than I all about the games appropriate to the occasion. You belong to the present, I to the past; you make the snow man now and here; I only tell about it from memory. We shall do better to go on with our modest studies, in which I can be of some help to you.

(7)   "From snow to hail is a short step, both being nothing but atmospheric vapor turned to ice by cold. But while snow is in delicate flakes, hail takes the form of hard pellets of ice called hailstones. These vary greatly in size, from that of a tiny pin-head to that of a pea, a plum, a pigeon's egg, and larger.

(8)   "Hail often does much harm. The icy pellets, hard as stone, in falling from the clouds gain speed enough to make them break window-panes, bruise the unfortunate person not under cover, and cut to pieces in a few minutes harvests, vineyards, and fruit-crops. It is nearly always in warm weather that hail falls, and as necessary conditions there must be a violent storm with flashes of lightning and peals of thunder.

(9)   "If on the one hand a hail-storm is to be regarded as a disaster, on the other a fall of snow is often to be welcomed as a blessing. Snow slowly saturates the earth with moisture that is of more lasting benefit than a rainfall. It also covers the fields with a mantle that affords protection from severe frost, so that the young shoots from seeds recently sown remain green and vigorous instead of being exposed to the deadly sting of the north wind.

(10)   "Snow plays still another part, and a very important one, a part having to do with the very existence of our streams. On account of the cold in high regions it snows more often on the mountains than in the plains. In our latitude peaks three thousand meters high, or more, are unvisited by rain. Every cloud borne to them by the wind deposits, instead of a shower of rain, a mantle of snow, and that in all seasons of the year, summer as well as winter.

(11)   "Driven by the wind or sliding down the steep slopes, this snow from the mountain-tops, renewed almost daily, collects in the neighboring valleys and piles up there in drifts hundreds of meters deep, which finally turn to ice as hard and clear as that of the pond where we go skating. In this way there are formed and maintained those masses of moving ice known as glaciers, immense reservoirs of frozen water which abound in all the larger mountain systems.

(12) "In its upper reaches, where the mountain peaks pierce the sky, the glacier is continually receiving fresh snow that comes sliding down the neighboring slopes, while in its lower course, farther down the valley, where the warmth is sufficient, the ice melts and gives rise to a stream which is soon added to by others from neighboring glaciers. In this way the largest rivers are started on their courses.

33. **Create a summary of "Snow" by writing the letters of three sentences into the summary boxes, in the correct order. The sentences should describe important events or ideas from the story.**

Ⓐ I only tell about it from memory. We shall do better to go on with our modest studies, in which I can be of some help to you.

Ⓑ From snow to hail is a short step, both being nothing but atmospheric vapor turned to ice by cold. But while snow is in delicate flakes, hail takes the form of hard pellets of ice called hailstones.

Ⓒ Snow has the same origin as rain: it comes from vapor in the atmosphere, especially from vapor rising from the surface of the sea.

Ⓓ Oh, how glorious is a holiday when there is snow on the ground! If I were to let myself go, how eloquent I could be on the subject!

Ⓔ Now is the time for dusting the back of a schoolmate with a well-directed snowball, which will bring a prompt reply.

Ⓕ Snow plays still another part, and a very important one, a part having to do with the very existence of our streams.

```
┌─────────────────────────────────────────────────┐
│ Summary 1                                         │
│                                                   │
│                                                   │
│                                                   │
│                                                   │
└─────────────────────────────────────────────────┘

┌─────────────────────────────────────────────────┐
│ Summary 2                                         │
│                                                   │
│                                                   │
│                                                   │
│                                                   │
└─────────────────────────────────────────────────┘

┌─────────────────────────────────────────────────┐
│ Summary 3                                         │
│                                                   │
│                                                   │
│                                                   │
│                                                   │
└─────────────────────────────────────────────────┘
```

LumosLearning.com   ▲

34.   How does the author's creation of the passage best explain snow?

Ⓐ The passage is broken into major sections.
Ⓑ The passage is created in chronological order.
Ⓒ The passage is created by separate paragraphs of key information.
Ⓓ The passage is created by separate sections with headings.

35.   **PART A**

After reading the cause in the box labeled cause, pick the correct letter that is the effect and write it in the box effect.

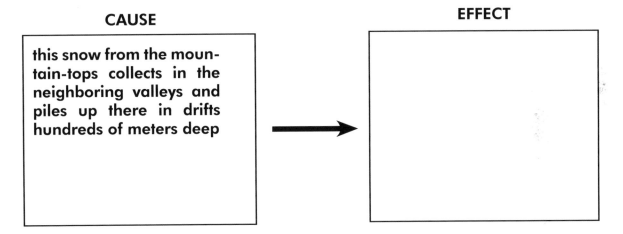

CAUSE

this snow from the mountain-tops collects in the neighboring valleys and piles up there in drifts hundreds of meters deep

EFFECT

Possible Effects

Ⓐ Drinkable water is found
Ⓑ Water hardens and freezes
Ⓒ Snowball fights occur
Ⓓ Hail falls after the snow hardens

PART B

Write the paragraph number from the passage above that best supports your answer in **PART A**.

Read "Snow in Town" and answer the questions that follow.

SNOW IN TOWN
By Rickman Mark

(1)   Nothing is quite so quiet and clean
As snow that falls in the night;
And is n't it jolly to jump from bed
And find the whole world white?

(2)   It lies on the window ledges,
It lies on the boughs of the trees,
While sparrows crowd at the kitchen door,
With a pitiful "If you please?"

(3)   It lies on the arm of the lamp-post,
Where the lighter's ladder goes,
And the policeman under it beats his arms,
And stamps—to feel his toes;

(4)   The butcher's boy is rolling a ball
To throw at the man with coals,
And old Mrs. Ingram has fastened a piece
Of flannel under her soles;

(5)   No sound there is in the snowy road
From the horses' cautious feet,
And all is hushed but the postman's knocks
Rat-tatting down the street,

(6)   Till men come round with shovels
To clear the snow away,—
What a pity it is that when it falls
They never let it stay!

(7)   And while we are having breakfast
Papa says, "Isn't it light?
And all because of the thousands of geese
The Old Woman plucked last night.

(8)   "And if you are good," he tells us,
"And attend to your A B C,
You may go in the garden and make a snow man
As big or bigger than me."

      LumosLearning.com

36. What type of language is used in Stanza 7 of the poem above?

  Ⓐ Onomatopoeia
  Ⓑ Simile
  Ⓒ Alliteration
  Ⓓ Metaphor

37. How does the formation of the actual passage of "Snow in Town" differ from the previous passage entitled "Snow"?

  Ⓐ The first passage is broken into stanzas and the second is broken into paragraphs.
  Ⓑ The first passage is broken into paragraphs and the second is broken into stanzas.
  Ⓒ The first passage is broken into stanzas and the second is broken into key sections.
  Ⓓ The first passage is broken into key sections and the second is broken into stanzas.

38. Both "Snow in Town" and "Snow" discuss the impact of a snowfall. Read the list of impacts and place the letter of each impact into the correct passage below.

  Ⓐ It lies on the arm of the lamp-post
  Ⓑ In this way the largest rivers are started on their courses.
  Ⓒ Snow, the schoolboy's favorite plaything
  Ⓓ Nothing is quite so quiet and clean
  Ⓔ Till men come round with shovels, to clear the snow away
  Ⓕ Everything will be hidden under a sheet of dazzling whiteness.

Snow in Town	Snow

End of Summative Assessment (SA) - 1

Summative Assessment (SA) - 1

Answer Key

Question No.	Answer	Related Lumos Online Workbook	CCSS
Unit 1			
1 Part A	A	A matter of attitude	RL.7.4
1 Part B	D	A matter of attitude	RL.7.4
2	A	Who or what?	RL.7.3
3	B	Prove it! (With evidence from the text)	RL.7.1
4	C	A matter of attitude	RL.7.4
5	C	What is it all about?; And the point of this is…?	RL.7.2
6	A, D, E, & F	What is it all about?; And the point of this is…?	RL.7.2
7	*	Say what you mean	W.7.3
8	C	One thing leads to another; When and where?	RL.7.3
9	D	How its made and what it means	RL.7.5
10	B	What a character!	RL.7.6
11	A	Figuring it out with context clues	L.7.4
Unit 2			
12 Part A	A	Getting technical	RI.7.4
12 Part B	C	Getting technical	RI.7.4
13	D	Getting technical	RI.7.4
14	B, C, and E	Get right to the point	RI.7.2
15 Part A	B	Getting technical	RI.7.4
15 Part B	A	How is it built? Analyzing structure	RI.7.5
16	D	Whats the authors angle?	RI.7.6
17	C, D, B, and A	Relationship between people and events	RI.7.3
18 Part A	C	Getting technical	RI.7.4
18 Part B	B	How is it built? Analyzing structure	RI.7.5
19	D	Relationship between people and events	RI.7.3
20	D and G	Relationship between people and events	RI.7.3
21	*	Getting from here to there - transitions; A picture is worth a thousand words	W.7.2

* See detailed explanation

LumosLearning.com

Question No.	Answer	Related Lumos Online Workbook	CCSS
22	C	Get right to the point	RI.7.2
23	A	How is it built? Analyzing structure	RI.7.5
24 Part A	C	Figuring it out with context clues	L.7.4
24 Part B	B	Figuring it out with context clues	L.7.4
25	A, B, and E	Whats the authors point?	RI.7.8
26 Part A	B	Relationship between people and events	RI.7.3
26 Part B	D	Relationship between people and events	RI.7.3
Unit 3			
27	A	Getting technical	RL.7.4
28	C	What a character!	RL.7.6
29	A	How its made and what it means	RL.7.5
30	B, C, and E	A matter of attitude	RL.7.4
31 Part A	C	Prove it! (With evidence from the text)	RL.7.1
31 Part B	D	Prove it! (With evidence from the text)	RL.7.1
32	*	Say what you mean	W.7.3
33	C, B, and E	Get right to the point	RI.7.2
34	C	How is it built? Analyzing structure	RI.7.5
35 Part A	B	Relationship between people and events	RI.7.3
35 Part B	Paragraph 11	Prove it! (With evidence from the text)	RI.7.1
36	D	A matter of attitude	RL.7.4
37	B	How is it built? Analyzing structure	RI.7.5
38	A, D, E	Equal? Alike? Different? Comparing authors	RI.7.9
	B, C, F		

* See detailed explanation

Summative Assessment (SA) - 1

Detailed Explanations

Question No.	Answer	Detailed Explanation
Unit 1		
1 Part A	A	Cunning means crafty or devious. Manipulative can also sometimes be cunning but strange is not so 'B' is incorrect.
1 Part B	D	The townspeople assumed she was cunning because they could not find the necklace anywhere and thought it to be hidden so well.
2	A	Because of the bolt of lightning, Martha was proven innocent once the bird's nest fell to the ground. The text mentions the bird's nest falling, but not the bird.
3	B	In the case of this story, the primary theme is that, in the end, justice will be serve.
4	C	The definition of illumined is to enlighten. In this case, the author is discussing how differently a person sees things once they have been enlightened.
5	C	The word was used as a way for the author to describe that illumined meant enlightened and not bright and cheery.
6	A, D, E, and F	These phrases each offer a different example of unjust moments.
7		See Rubric Page No. 10 & 11
8	C	The flickering electricity and single, solitary light create a mysterious atmosphere in that paragraph.
9	D	Subtitles offer clarity to the content of the story. In this case, this would allow the reader to know what the story is about.
10	B	Throughout the story, the reader sees younger David's concern and fear. He is very cautious. On the other hand, older David is very confident in his actions and speech.
11	A	"A smart cookie" can be classified as a metaphor which occurs when a phrase is applied to an item. In this case, a cookie is not literally smart, but the overall phrase has meaning.
Unit 2		
12 Part A	A	Primitive means not developed or coming from the early time of history

LumosLearning.com   ▲

Question No.	Answer	Detailed Explanation
12 Part B	C	Living in tents, riding camels as transportation, and fighting with bows and arrows is often thought of as the early times in history. We would consider that to be a primitive way of life.
13	D	Although each of the other answers was mentioned in the text, none of them are the primary, or major, reason inventions are created. They are made as a way to solve everyday problems or to see if something can be done.
14	B, C, and E	While each of the phrases are mentioned in the passage, only B, C, and E are used as descriptors of inventions. Each of those terms can be found in paragraph 3.
15 Part A	B	Awkward means difficult to deal with.
15 Part B	A	The way the author describes how others relate to Einstein indicate he was difficult to deal with.
16	D	Although the text does not specifically say, the reader can.
17	C, D, B, and A	Although dates are not specifically mentioned in the given details, careful reading of the passage indicates this is the order they occurred.
18 Part A	C	The definition of ludicrous is so unreasonable it could be amusing; absurd has a similar meaning which makes it a synonym.
18 Part B	B	The idea that people would want their own computers was considered extremely unreasonable to most people of that time.
19	D	Einsten's quote is closest to one that Jobs might agree with. Jobs recognized the absolute potential computers had for people when they were combined with human ingenuity and needs.
20	D and G	Both Jobs and Einstein dropped out of school at early ages indicating anyone can invent new ideas and objects, not just those with advanced degrees.
21		See Rubric Page No. 10 & 11
22	C	Molly Pitcher remained calm throughout the entire battle. This allowed her to make strategic decisions like fetching water for the men and taking charge of her husband's canon once he had fallen.
23	A	By using quotations only by Molly Pitcher, the author allows the reader a deeper understanding of what Molly was trying to say. It also adds authenticity to each of those moments.
24 Part A	C	The meaning of rebuke is sharp disapproval.
24 Part B	B	Washington's disapproval of the General was so strong, the man turned white as a sheet.

Question No.	Answer	Detailed Explanation
25	A, B, and E	Although each of the statements listed come directly from the text, these three are the primary descriptions of her courageous behavior that earned her the title of Captain.
26 Part A	B	Because Molly brought water to the soldiers, they were able to continue the fight.
26 Part B	D	This statement offers evidence of how her actions influenced the men.
Unit 3		
27	A	Repine means to fret or to express discontent
28	C	Although the poem begins with a description of a dark, dreary, windy day in nature, it turns to a discussion of a dreary life and how there can be a little hope in the midst of the darkness.
29	A	The poem begins with a description of the physical world but then it turns to a personal reflection.
30	B, C, and E	Each of these phrases show the best examples of imagery in the poem.
31 Part A	C	The author is talking to himself through the poem, both his current self and his past thoughts.
31 Part B	D	Throughout the poem, the author talks about "my thoughts" which shows how he is talking about himself.
32		See Rubric Page No. 10 & 11
33	C, B, and E	These are the primary events in the story, in the order they occurred. The others are events; however, they are not the most important parts of the passage.
34	C	The author uses storytelling as the primary means of delivery; therefore, the passage is written in paragraph form. Each paragraph contains key information about snow.
35 Part A	B	Once the snow collects in the valleys, it collects and hardens. Although the collected water may eventually become drinkable water, it is not explicitly mentioned in the text.
35 Part B	Paragraph 11	This paragraph mentions snow collecting, hardening, and then freezing.
36	D	The phrase "And all because of the thousands of geese, The Old Woman plucked last night," is used to describe the snow. Because snow is not actually made from plucked feathers of geese, that phrase is not literally applicable to snow.
37	B	The first passage is an informational piece broken into paragraphs of information. The second is a poem broken into several stanzas.

LumosLearning.com ▲

Question No.	Answer	Detailed Explanation
38	A, D, E	These three impacts are direct statements from the poem.
	B, C, F	These three impacts come directly from the passage on Snow.

Summative Assessment (SA) - 2

Here are some reminders for when you are taking the Grade 7 ELA Summative Assessment (SA)

- You may look back at the reading passage as often as you want.
- Read each question carefully and think about the answer. Then completely fill in the circle next to your choice.
- If you do not know the answer to a question, go on to the next question and come back to the skipped question later.

The Secret of Everyday Things
Fire
by Jean Henri Fabre

(1) "We do not know how man first procured fire. Did he take advantage of some blaze started by a thunderbolt, or did he kindle his first firebrand in the crater of a volcano? No one can tell. Whatever may have been its source, man has enjoyed the use of fire from the earliest times; but as the means of relighting it if it went out were very imperfect or even lacking altogether, the utmost care was taken to maintain it, and a few live coals were always kept over from one day to the next.

(2) "So calamitous would have been the simultaneous extinction of the fires in all the dwellings that, in order to guard against such a disaster, the priesthood took fire under its special protection. In ancient Rome, many centuries ago, an order of priestesses called Vestals was charged with the guarding of the sacred fire night and day. The unfortunate one who let it go out was punished with horrible torture: she was buried alive!"

(3) "Did they really bury her alive for letting the fire go out?" asked Jules.

(4) "Yes, my boy. This terrible punishment inflicted on the keepers of the fire shows you the importance they attached to keeping at least one hearth alight so that others could be kindled from it."

(5) "One of our matches that we buy at a cent a hundred," said Claire, "would have saved the life of the careless Vestal."

(6)   "Yes, to abolish those barbarous severities it needed only a match, a thing which unfortunately was at that time unknown.

(7)   "Many centuries passed before it was discovered how to procure fire easily. In my young days, when I was about your age, keeping coals alive to be used for relighting the fire next day was still the rule in the country. In the evening before the family went to bed, the embers were carefully covered with hot ashes to prevent their burning out and to keep them alive. If, despite this precaution, the hearth was cold next morning, someone had to hasten to the nearest neighbor's to borrow some fire, that is to say a few live coals, which were carried home in an old wooden shoe to keep the wind from blowing them away."

(8)   "But I should think the old wooden shoe would have caught fire," said Emile.

(9)   "No, for care was taken to put a layer of ashes in first. I have told you how some children would put a few ashes in the hollow of their hand, and on the ashes lay live coals. They carried fire thus just as you would carry a handful of sugar-plums.

(10)   "The layer of ashes arrested the heat of the embers and prevented its reaching the hand. Remember what I have already told you about the poor conducting power of ashes, their refusal to transmit heat, a characteristic they have in common with all powdery substances. The little fire-borrowers knew that well enough."

(11)   "But who taught them to do it that way?" asked Emile.

(12)   "The great teacher of all things, necessity. Caught without shovel or wooden shoe, some one of them, knowing this peculiarity of ashes in arresting heat, made use of the ingenious device I have described, and his example was sooner or later followed by others.

(13)   "Fire-producing devices are, as a rule, based on the principle that heat is generated by friction. We all know that we can warm our hands by rubbing them against each other."

(14)   "That's what I always do in winter when my hands are frozen from making snowballs," said Jules.

(15)   "That is one of the oldest illustrations of the effect of friction, and I will add another. Hold this round-headed metal button by the shank and rub it briskly on the wood of the table; it will become warm enough to produce a decided feeling on the skin."

(16)   Claire took the button, rubbed it on the wood of the table, and then applied it quickly to her hand, uttering a little cry of surprise and even of pain as she did so.

(17)   "Oh, how hot the button is, Uncle!" she exclaimed. "If I had rubbed any longer I should have scorched my hand."

(18)   "It is by similar means that certain savage tribes procured and still procure fire. They twirl very rapidly between their hands a slender stick of hard wood with its pointed end inserted in a cavity hollowed in soft and very inflammable wood. If the friction is brisk enough and the operation properly carried out, the soft wood catches fire. This process, I admit, would fail of success in our hands for lack of skill."

(19)   "For my part," said Marie, "if I had nothing but a pointed stick and a piece of wood with a hole in it for lighting a fire, I should despair of ever managing it."

(20)   "I should not even try it," Claire confessed, "it seems so difficult, although the button that I rubbed came near burning me."

(21)   "What would be impossible for us is mere play for the natives of Australia. The operator sits on the ground, holding between his feet the piece of wood with the little hole, and twirling the pointed stick rapidly between his hands he soon obtains a spark with which he kindles a few dry leaves.

(22)   "Even in our own country you may see, in any wood-turner's shop, this friction process employed successfully. To obtain the brown ornamental lines on certain objects turned in a lathe, the operator presses with some force the point of a bit of wood on the piece in rapid rotation. The line thus impressed by friction begins to smoke in a few moments, and soon becomes carbonized.

(23)   "I pass on to other methods of producing fire. Iron and steel, especially the latter, if rubbed against a very hard stone give out sparks made by tiny scales of metal that become detached and are sufficiently heated to turn red and burn in the air. Thus the scissors-grinder's revolving stone, although constantly moistened with water, throws out a shower of sparks under the steel knife or other tool that is being sharpened. In like manner the cobblestone struck by the horse's iron shoe emits sudden and brilliant flashes.

(24)   "The common flint-and-steel apparatus acts in the same way. It consists of a piece of steel that is struck against the edge of a very hard stone called silex or flint. Particles of steel are detached from the metal and, made red-hot by the friction, set fire to the tinder. This latter is a very combustible substance obtained by cutting a large mushroom into thin slices and drying them, the mushroom being of the kind known as touchwood, which grows on tree trunks."

             LumosLearning.com

1.   **PART A**

What is the meaning of the word <u>calamitous</u> as it is used in paragraph two of the passage above?

Ⓐ Wholesome
Ⓑ Catastrophic
Ⓒ Advantageous
Ⓓ Lucky

PART B

What evidence do you have from the text to support your answer in PART A?

Ⓐ To abolish those barbarous severities it needed only a match, a thing which unfortunately was at that time unknown.
Ⓑ We do not know how man first procured fire.
Ⓒ In order to guard against such a disaster, the priesthood took fire under its special protection.
Ⓓ If, despite this precaution, the hearth was cold next morning, someone had to hasten to the nearest neighbor's to borrow some fire.

2.   The boxes below contain various ways fire can be made according to the text. Select the missing method from the list and place the letter in the last box.

Ⓐ Mushroom
Ⓑ Igniting buttons
Ⓒ Twirling twine between feet
Ⓓ Matches

Method 1	Method 2	Method 3
Protecting Embers	Thunderbolt	Friction

Method 4
??

3.   How is the importance of fire stressed throughout the passage?

Ⓐ Man's ability to cook food and boil water is described.
Ⓑ Descriptions are given of what happened to those who let the fire burn down.
Ⓒ The ability to protect burning embers with a layer of ash is described.
Ⓓ The various methods of creating fire are described in such detail that any one can start a fire.

LumosLearning.com

▼

Read the passage and answer the questions that follow.

The Girl Who Sat by the Ashes
by Padraic Colum

FIRE FOR THE KING'S SON

(1)   In the morning early she rose up, opened wide the door and let the Goats go through. She milked a little from the brown Goat and drank the milk for her breakfast. Then she let the seven Goats go by themselves off to the high places and the rocky places.

(2)   She went down to the stream and she washed her face and her hands. Then she stood on the bank and the two starlings flew down, lighting one on each shoulder, and they began to sing to her. The song they sang was of the Little Brown Jug that she washed every day and left in the center place on the dresser:

(3)   Little Brown Jug,
Don't I love thee?
Bright and brown
Like a kept penny!

I'll fill thee with honey,
I'll fill thee with spice,
I'll border thee with flowers
Of every device.

I'll not let befall thee
A chip or a crack;
I'll leave pewter below thee,
And delph at thy back.

I'll fill thee with spice,
And I'll fill thee with honey,
And I'd not part with thee
For a kettle-full of money.

Little Brown Jug,
Don't I love thee?
Bright and brown
Like a kept penny.

And when the starlings had sung to her, Girl-go-with-the-Goats was not as heavy at heart as she had been before.

(4)   After a very busy day, her stepmother, Dame Dale was at the door. She told Girl-go-with-the-Goats to eat her dinner off the board at the gable end of the house and then go and bring back the seven Goats from the high places and the rocky places.

(5)   She ate her dinner of bread and milk and an egg. Then she brought the Goats home. Her step-mother told her she need not milk them as she had to go to a certain place before the dark of the night came down.

And where had she to go to? To the Forge in the Forest. And what had she to go for? For a pot of fire, no less.

(6)   For all that morning Buttercup and Berry-bright, after washing their hands with new milk, sat dizening themselves as before. And Dame Dale, being wearied from her journey, stayed in bed. The consequence of it all was that the fire on the hearth had gone out, and there was no way now of kindling a fire. And the only place to get fire was at the Forge in the Forest which was more like a moorland than a forest because all the trees had been cut down.

(7)   And now Girl-go-with-the-Goats was bidden take a pot in her hands and go to the Forge in the Forest for fire for her step-mother's hearth. She started off, and no sooner had she turned the loaning when the starlings again flew down on her shoulders. And as she went along the path through the wood the two starlings sang to her; whatever she thought of, that they sang to her. She came out on the moorland and when she went a furlong she saw the black forge. Two Dwarfs with earrings in their ears were within. They took two pieces of glowing wood out of their fire and put them in her pot.

(8)   Back she went, hurrying now across the moorland because dark clouds were gathering. As she went along the path through the wood the starlings on her shoulders twittered their nesting song. The wood was dark around her and she hurried, hurried on.

And on the outskirts of the wood she saw a youth gathering kindlings for a fire. She came face to face with him and she knew him, He was the King's son.

(9)   She put down the pot and at once she began gathering kindlings with him. She brought them where he was bringing his. She laid hers down and built up a fire for him.

"This the night when, according to my father's councillors, I have to sleep on the moorland," said the King's son. He searched in his wallet. "I had flint and steel," he said, "but I have lost the flint and steel that was to make my fire."

▼

(10) "I have embers," said Girl-go-with-the-Goats. She took the burning embers out of the pot and put them under the wood. A fire began to crackle.

"Leave me now," said the King's son.

"Would you not give me an ember out of the fire I have kindled?" said Girl-go-with-the-Goats.

"I will give you an ember, but not two embers," said the King's son.

(11) She took an ember from the fire. It was not a weighty ember like one of the two the Dwarfs had given her. It was a light and a waning ember. She took it and put it in the pot, thinking she would find kindling on the wayside.

(12) She went on and on but she found no kindling. And when she looked into her pot again the ember had died out. What was she to do? She walked back, and she saw the fire she had lighted blazing up. She saw the King's son standing beside the fire. She went nearer, but she could hear his voice as he said to her, "I will give you an ember, but not two embers." She was afraid to go near him and have him speak to her again.

4. **What is a synonym of the word <u>waning</u> mean as it is used in paragraph 12 of the passage?**

   Ⓐ **Diminishing**
   Ⓑ **Strengthening**
   Ⓒ **Brightening**
   Ⓓ **Lightning**

5. **Create a sequence of events as they happened in the story. Write the letter of each event, in order, into the boxes below.**

   Ⓐ **Her step-mother told her she need not milk them as she had to go to a certain place before the dark of the night came down.**
   Ⓑ **She saw the King's son standing beside the fire. She went nearer, but she could hear his voice as he said to her, "I will give you an ember, but not two embers."**
   Ⓒ **And now Girl-go-with-the-Goats was bidden take a pot in her hands and go to the Forge in the Forest for fire for her step-mother's hearth.**
   Ⓓ **She took the burning embers out of the pot and put them under the wood. A fire began to crackle.**

Event 1	Event 2	Event 3	Event 4

6. What theme is common between both *The Girl Who Sat by the Ashes and The Secret of Everyday Things: Fire?*

    (A) Fire helps one accomplish important tasks
    (B) Fire is the most important element
    (C) Fire is essential and worth protecting
    (D) Fire comes and goes but is always able to be started when necessary.

7. In both *The Girl Who Sat by the Ashes and The Secret of Everyday Things: Fire*, fire plays a critical role. Write an essay about a situation you can imagine, or have witnessed, when fire played a significant role.

Read the passage and answer the questions that follow.

The Top and the Ball
Adapted from Hans Christian Andersen by Miss C. W. Mingins

(1) A Top and a Ball lay together in a drawer with some other toys. The Top said to the Ball: "Why should we not be the very best of friends, and play together, as we are lying here in the same drawer?"

(2) But the Ball, who was covered with Morocco leather, and thought she was very fine, would not reply.

(3) The next day the little boy to whom the Top belonged painted it in red and yellow, and drove a brass nail into the head. This looked really beautiful when the Top spun around.

(4) "Just look at me," he said to the Ball. "Am I not pretty, too? Let us be companions. We should be very happy, for you jump and I dance, and there would be no happier play-mates than we two."

(5) "Do you think so?" said the Ball. "Perhaps you do not know that I am made of Morocco, and have a cork in my body!"

(6) "Yes; but I am made of mahogany," said the Top. "The Mayor himself turned me, for he has a turning-lathe of his own. He enjoys making tops to please the children."

(7) "Is that really so?" asked the Ball.

(8) "Just as true as that I can spin," said the Top.

(9) The Ball looked at the pleasant, happy little Top and said: "But I want to be the swallow's playmate. Whenever I fly up into the air, he calls from the tree-top: 'Will you, will you?' and I have said 'Yes,' but I will always remember you, Top."

(10) "Oh, very well," said the Top, "but you can't play with the swallow, and you can come with me; still, do as you wish."

(11) The next day the Ball was taken out of the drawer, and the Top saw her flying high up in the air—she seemed almost like a bird. Whenever she returned to the earth, she gave a little jump just as she touched the ground. Perhaps that was because she wanted to fly again, or because she had a cork in her body.

 LumosLearning.com ▼

(12)   But one time, when she was sent flying in the air, she did not come back; and, although the little boy hunted and hunted, she could not be found—she was lost.

(13)   "I know where she is," thought the Top. "She has gone to the swallow's nest; she has gone to stay with the swallow."

(14)   The Top was very lonely. He thought and thought about the Ball, and, although he spun around and hummed his pretty song, he was always wanting her. Many days and weeks passed by, and the Top was growing old. His red and yellow paint had worn off, and the little boy did not play with him as much as he used to. One day the Top was gilded all over. He looked like a gold top. The little boy thought him more beautiful than ever before. The Top spun and hummed and jumped about, but all at once he went too high, and was lost. They searched everywhere, but no one could find the gold Top. Where had he gone?

(15)   He had fallen into the trash can, where all sorts of garbage was. "Well, well," said the Top; "this is a queer place! All my gilding will be spoiled, and I cannot even spin down here in the dark. And the little boy will be lonely."

(16)   Just then he saw something round and dirty, like a withered apple—but the round thing began to talk!

(17)   "Oh, dear," it said; "I have been lying here in this dirty place for weeks, with no one good enough for me to play with. I wanted to live with the swallow, but I fell in here, and I am very beautiful, for I am made of Morocco leather and I have a cork in my body."

(18)   Then the Top knew it was the Ball, lost so long ago. Just then came a maid to clear out the dust bin. The first thing she saw was the Top. She took it to the little boy again, and both the Top and the little boy were happy. But the Ball was thrown away. The Top never spoke of the Ball. He thought her a silly little Ball, after all—for it is better always to think of others, and not of yourself.

8.   **Part A.**

What does the word <u>gilded</u> mean as used in paragraph 14?

Ⓐ cut into pieces
Ⓑ wrapped with tape
Ⓒ painted red
Ⓓ painted gold

Part B.

Which detail from the story best supports your answer to Part A?

Ⓐ The Top spun and hummed and jumped
Ⓑ His red and yellow paint
Ⓒ He looked like a gold top.
Ⓓ the Top was growing old.

9.   **Part A.**

Why doesn't the Ball want to play with the Top?

Ⓐ She thinks the Top is not a very friendly toy.
Ⓑ She doesn't think she is good enough to have such a friend as the Top.
Ⓒ She thinks she is too pretty and fine for the Top.
Ⓓ She is very shy.

Part B.

Which detail from the story best supports your answer to Part A?

Ⓐ But the Ball, who was covered with Morocco leather, and thought she was very fine, would not reply.
Ⓑ she wanted to fly again, because she had a cork in her body.
Ⓒ "Yes; but I am made of mahogany," said the Top.
Ⓓ I have been lying here in this dirty place for weeks.

LumosLearning.com   ▼

10.   **Part A.**

What is the importance of paragraph 17?

Ⓐ It explains why the Ball did not like the Top.
Ⓑ It shows that the Ball did not change, even after she had been in the trash can for weeks.
Ⓒ It describes how the Ball went to live with the swallows.
Ⓓ It tells about the Ball's exciting adventure in the trash can.

Part B.

Which detail from the story best supports your answer to Part A?

Ⓐ He saw something round and dirty, like a withered apple.
Ⓑ But the Ball was thrown away.
Ⓒ "Well, well," said the Top; "this is a queer place!"
Ⓓ I have been lying here in this dirty place for weeks, with no one good enough for me to play with.

11.   Choose 3 sentences to summarize the events in the passage. Write the letters of the sentences in order in the box.

Ⓐ A lonely boy was looking for some toys to play with.
Ⓑ The ball was impressed with her own beauty and thought the top was not good enough to play with her.
Ⓒ The top ended up in the trash can as well. He was rescued, but the ball was thrown away.
Ⓓ The maid felt sorry for the top, but did not care about the ball.
Ⓔ A top asked a ball to be his friend and playmate.
Ⓕ The ball wanted to fly up high and be with the swallows, but ended up in the trash can.

Unit 2

Read the passage below and answer the questions that follow.

America First—100 Stories from Our History
by Lawton B. Evans

OLD HICKORY

(1)   ANDREW JACKSON is one of the most picturesque characters in American history. He was born of Scotch-Irish parents on the border-line between North and South Carolina. His father died about the time he was born, and his mother had to support her three boys by spinning flax.

(2)   Jackson grew up to be a tall, slender lad, with red hair and a freckled face. He was very wild, quick-tempered, and mischievous. He had many quarrels with his companions, and many fights, but, at home, he was devoted to his mother, and showed kindness to the horses and other animals on the farm. He was a fearless rider, and all his life owned fine horses.

(3)   When Jackson was fourteen years of age, the Revolution was still in progress. The British army had swept through the neighborhood of his home, and the boy had seen his relatives and neighbors suffering and dying.

(4)   The local church was used as a hospital, and Jackson's mother often went there to nurse the sick and wounded. Andrew and his brother Robert ran errands for her, and were in and out of the church so often that they soon became familiar with the horrors of war.

(5)   At one time, Andrew and his brother were taken prisoners by the British, and were confined in the house of their own cousin. The English officers had everything they wished, and one of them ordered Jackson to clean his muddy boots.

(6)   Andrew replied, "I am a prisoner of war, and not a servant or a slave. You may clean them yourself."

(7)   This enraged the British officer to such an extent that he struck at the boy with his sword, wounding him on his head and hand. Jackson carried the scars with him all his life. Robert also received rough treatment from the brutal officers.

(8)   The boys were carried forty miles away, to a prison camp, and not allowed any food or water. There, smallpox broke out, and both boys were quite sick with it. Their mother secured their release, but Robert, suffering from wounds and fever, died two days after he reached home, and Andrew was ill for many weeks. Before he was quite well his mother also died.

             ▼

(9)   At seventeen years of age, he began to study law. When he was twenty-one, he moved to Tennessee, and became a prominent lawyer in that new and wild country. In his efforts to preserve law and order among the frontiersmen and adventurers of that section, he had many personal difficulties. He was hot-tempered and a good shot, and frontier life was rough.

(10)   One day, when he was at a public dinner, some of his friends began to quarrel at the other end of the table from where Jackson was sitting. He immediately sprang upon the table, and strode along it, scattering the dishes and glasses as he went. Thrusting his hand behind him, he clicked his snuff-box. Thinking he was about to draw a pistol, the guests ran out in haste, crying in alarm, "Don't shoot, Mr. Jackson! Don't shoot!"

(11)   Once, when Jackson was driving along the road, he was stopped by some drunken wagoners, who told him to dance, or they would cowhide him. Jackson coolly said, "I cannot dance in these heavy boots. Let me get my slippers out of my bag."

(12)   To this the wagoners agreed, but, instead of slippers, he drew forth two big pistols. Pointing them at the wagoners, he said, "Now dance yourselves, or I will fill you full of bullets." The wagoners danced the best they could, while Jackson roared with laughter.

(13)   During the War of 1812, Jackson did great service as a soldier. He fought against the Indians in the South, and was prominent at the battle of New Orleans. A band of Creeks attacked Fort Mimms, in southern Alabama, and killed four or five hundred white people. Tennessee raised a body of troops to go after the Creeks and punish them. Jackson was chosen Commander.

(14)   He was in bed at the time, suffering from wounds he had received in a quarrel two weeks before. His physician ordered him to stay where he was, but Jackson arose, put his arm in a sling, and, though almost fainting from weakness and loss of blood, he mounted his horse and started on the campaign. He was gone eight months, and the Creeks were severely punished.

(15)   Once, during the campaign, some soldiers grew mutinous because food was scarce, and they threatened to leave. Jackson, with his arm in a sling, rode up to them, and, taking his pistol in his free hand, said, "By the eternal, I will shoot the first man that moves." The soldiers knew he would do it, and there was no further trouble.

(16)   His endurance during this campaign earned for him the name of "Old Hickory," because he was so tough; and because, though he would often bend, he would not break. In appearance, he was tall, erect, and spare, with dark blue eyes and heavy eyebrows. All through life his temper was fiery, and easily aroused when he was opposed.

12. **PART A**

In paragraph 14, Jackson is described as having a <u>quarrel</u>. What does that word mean as it is used in the passage?

Ⓐ Peaceful agreement
Ⓑ Discussion
Ⓒ Ugly alteration
Ⓓ Angry argument

PART B

What evidence exists in the passage above that best supports your answer in PART A? Write the letter of your selection in the box below.

Ⓐ During the War of 1812, Jackson did great service as a soldier. He fought against the Indians in the South, and was prominent at the battle of New Orleans.
Ⓑ Tennessee raised a body of troops to go after the Creeks and punish them. Jackson was chosen Commander.
Ⓒ He was in bed at the time, suffering from wounds he had received in a quar rel two weeks before.
Ⓓ Once, during the campaign, some soldiers grew mutinous because food was scarce, and they threatened to leave. Jackson, with his arm in a sling, rode up to them, and, taking his pistol in his free hand, said, "By the eternal, I will shoot the first man that moves."

13. Create a summary of *America First—100 Stories from Our History: OLD HICK-ORY* by writing the letters of three sentences into the summary boxes, in the correct order. The sentences should describe important events or ideas from the story.

 LumosLearning.com

Ⓐ His endurance during this campaign earned for him the name of "Old Hickory," because he was so tough; and because, though he would often bend, he would not break.

Ⓑ During the War of 1812, Jackson did great service as a soldier. He fought against the Indians in the South, and was prominent at the battle of New Orleans.

Ⓒ He was in bed at the time, suffering from wounds he had received in a quarrel two weeks before.

Ⓓ At one time, Andrew and his brother were taken prisoners by the British, and were confined in the house of their own cousin.

Ⓔ At seventeen years of age, he began to study law.
One day, when he was at a public dinner, some of his friends began to quar rel at the other end of the table from where Jackson was sitting.

Summary 1

Summary 2

Summary 3

---

14. Paragraph 16 of the passage above explains where Jackson's nickname came from. Reading the description of that name, what can you conclude about hickory wood?

Ⓐ It bends but does not break easily.
Ⓑ It is extremely fragile.
Ⓒ It is the heartiest and strongest wood around.
Ⓓ It is the best wood for making items.

Read "Fifty Famous People : The Young Scout" and answer the questions that follow.

Fifty Famous People
by James Baldwin

THE YOUNG SCOUT

(1)   WHEN Andrew Jackson was a little boy he lived with his mother in South Carolina. He was eight years old when he heard about the ride of Paul Revere and the famous fight at Lexington.

(2)   It was then that the long war, called the Revolutionary War, began. The king's soldiers were sent into every part of the country. The people called them the British. Some called them "red-coats."

(3)   There was much fighting; and several great battles took place between the British and the Americans.

(4)   At last Charleston, in South Carolina, was taken by the British. Andrew Jackson was then a tall white-haired boy, thirteen years old.

(5)   "I am going to help drive those red-coated British out of the country," he said to his mother.

(6)   Then, without another word, he mounted his brother's little farm horse and rode away. He was not old enough to be a soldier, but he could be a scout—and a good scout he was.

(7)   He was very tall—as tall as a man. He was not afraid of anything. He was strong and ready for every duty.

(8)   One day as he was riding through the woods, some British soldiers saw him. They quickly surrounded him and made him their prisoner.

(9)   "Come with us," they said, "and we will teach you that the king's soldiers are not to be trifled with."

(10)   They took him to the British camp.

(11)   "What is your name, young rebel?" said the British captain.

(12)   "Andy Jackson."

(13)   "Well, Andy Jackson, get down here and clean the mud from my boots."

© Lumos Information Services 2015   LumosLearning.com   ▼

(14) Andrew's gray eyes blazed as he stood up straight and proud before the haughty captain.

(15) "Sir," he said, "I am a prisoner of war, and demand to be treated as such."

(16) "You rebel!" shouted the captain. "Down with you, and clean those boots at once."

(17) The slim, tall boy seemed to grow taller, as he answered, "I'll not be the servant of any Englishman that ever lived."

(18) The captain was very angry. He drew his sword to hit the boy with its flat side. Andrew threw out his hand and received an ugly gash across the knuckles.

(19) Some other officers, who had seen the whole affair, cried out to the captain, "Shame! He is a brave boy. He deserves to be treated as a gentleman."

(20) Andrew was not held long as a prisoner. The British soldiers soon returned to Charleston, and he was allowed to go home.

(21) In time, Andrew Jackson became a very great man. He was elected to Congress, he was chosen judge of the supreme court of Tennessee, he was appointed general in the army, and lastly he was for eight years the president of the United States.

15. **In line 9 from the passage above, explain what the word <u>trifled</u> means.**

   Ⓐ **Danced**
   Ⓑ **Played**
   Ⓒ **Fought**
   Ⓓ **Claimed**

16. **You have read two different accounts of Jackson's capture by the British when he was a boy, one in _Fifty Famous People: THE YOUNG SCOUT_ and one in _America First – 100 Stories from Our History: OLD HICKORY_. Listed below are several key pieces of the descriptions. Select the letters of the descriptions and the write the letters in the correct boxes below. Some letters may be used in both accounts and some may not be used at all.**

Ⓐ The British ordered him to clean the mud from his boots.

Ⓑ "Sir," he said, "I am a prisoner of war, and demand to be treated as such."

Ⓒ "I am going to help drive those red-coated British out of the country," he said to his mother.

Ⓓ Andrew replied, "I am a prisoner of war, and not a servant or a slave. You may clean them yourself."

Ⓔ Jackson was struck on the head and hands and had scars from the incident.

Ⓕ Jackson's stubbornness helped him survive captivity.

OLD HICKORY	THE YOUNG SCOUT

17. Why was Jackson considered to be a good scout when he was young?

Ⓐ In time, Andrew Jackson became a very great man.

Ⓑ He stood up straight and proud before the haughty captain.

Ⓒ He stood up straight and proud before the haughty captain.

Ⓓ He was not afraid of anything. He was strong and ready for every duty.

18. You have read three different accounts of Andrew Jackson, each listing their own descriptions of his character. In the space below, write an essay picking the most important characteristic described that is needed to be a successful President. Your essay does not have to be limited to Jackson or early Presidents; it can include modern examples and descriptions.

    LumosLearning.com   ▼

Read "The Growth of Basketball" and answer the questions that follow.

The Growth of Basketball
Author Unknown

(1)   The origins of many games and sports are lost in history. No one knows who the first person to play tag or chess was. There are no photos of the first baseball or hockey game. The rules for football developed out of rugby and other earlier games. But one modern sport has a very clear beginning.

(2)   James Naismith was born in Canada in 1861. When he got a job at the YMCA Training School in Springfield, Massachusetts, he was asked to invent a game. It had to be something that kept students physically active, but could be played indoors -- because students stayed inside most of the long, cold New England winters.

(3)   On Dec. 21, 1891, Naismith showed his class the new game he had created out of five basic ideas and thirteen rules. He put two peach baskets up, one at each end of the court. There were nine players on each team, and they used a soccer ball. The bottoms of the peach baskets were intact. Whenever someone threw the ball into a basket, a student would climb a ladder to get the ball out. The player with the ball could not move – he had to pass it or shoot it. Dribbling was not invented until later.

(4)   The game began to catch on. By 1906, the game looked a bit more like it does today. It featured metal hoops with nets and backboards. Basketball was first featured in the Olympics in 1936 – and the game was played outside, on dirt, in bad weather. As time went on, basketball grew in popularity in the U.S. Two large leagues – the National Basketball Association (NBA), and the American Basketball Association (ABA) both flourished in the U.S. The NBA was the more traditional and better-known league, but the ABA had great flair. The NBA had established teams like the Boston Celtics and the Los Angeles Lakers, but the ABA had a red-white-and-blue ball, high-flying players, and entertainingly wild and colorful uniforms. The two leagues merged in 1976, bringing some of the showmanship of the ABA to the more formal NBA.

(5)   The result was a combined league that was poised, ready for greater growth. What it needed were some exciting rivalries and great players to bring it to the next level. In the 1980's, the league got both of these. The two best-known teams, the Celtics and Lakers, once again rose to the top of the league. And, they featured two players – Magic Johnson and Larry Bird – who were so outstanding and entertaining that people who had not been fans before began to take notice.

(6)   One more player pushed the league from national success to international superstardom in the late 1980's and early 1990's – Michael Jordan. Arguably the best player in the history of the game, Jordan was exactly what the NBA needed.
But that was on the court. Behind the scenes, the NBA and the game of basketball in general benefited from the remarkable leadership of a man few people know.

(7)   David Stern was chosen as the NBA's Commissioner in 1984. Like James Naismith, he was not much of an athlete. He was a short man who wore glasses and never played the game well. But Stern is a terrific businessman. He was hired at a time when many of the teams in the league were in trouble financially. Although big-city teams, which had large fan bases, were managing well, many smaller-market teams were barely surviving.

(8)   Fans loved the superstars on the court, but they were turned off by players' behavior off the court, such as drug use and other scandals. Stern immediately instituted new tough-on-drugs policies and used brilliant marketing techniques. The NBA has grown five times as wealthy as it was when Stern first became Commissioner, and it has done so at the international level. At Stern's insistence, NBA games are shown on TV regularly in dozens of other countries, and the best international players now come to play in the NBA as a result. NBA teams also play at least one game a year in a foreign country. With the NBA and their own leagues, countries all over the world are playing and watching basketball more than ever before.

19.   Part A.

How did David Stern improve the NBA?

Ⓐ He put in place stronger penalties for drug use and found better ways to "sell" basketball to the public.
Ⓑ He required players to practice more and coaches to be tougher.
Ⓒ He recruited some friends in Hollywood to make a movie about basketball.
Ⓓ He made all NBA employees take a test to determine their knowledge of the game.

Part B

Which detail in the passage provides the best evidence to the answer in Part A?

Ⓐ Many smaller-market teams were barely surviving.
Ⓑ David Stern was chosen as the NBA's Commissioner in 1984. Like James Naismith, he was not much of an athlete.
Ⓒ Stern immediately instituted new tough-on-drugs policies and used brilliant marketing techniques.
Ⓓ Fans loved the superstars on the court, but they were turned off by players' behavior off the court.

20. **Part A.**

What is the main idea of this passage?

Ⓐ The origin of basketball is more mysterious than that of other sports.
Ⓑ Basketball is a great game for those who can't play baseball or football.
Ⓒ David Stern did a lot of good things for the game of basketball.
Ⓓ Basketball is a game that was invented by a YMCA worker and has grown into an international sport.

Part B.

Which **two** details from the passage best support your answer to Part A?

Ⓐ Arguably the best player in the history of the game, Jordan was exactly what the NBA needed.
Ⓑ On Dec. 21, 1891, Naismith showed his class the new game he had created out of five basic ideas and thirteen rules.
Ⓒ The two leagues merged in 1976, bringing some of the showmanship of the ABA to the more formal NBA.
Ⓓ With the NBA and their own leagues, countries all over the world are playing and watching basketball more than ever before.

21. Which **two statements** describe the difference between the ABA and the NBA? Write them in the box.

Ⓐ The NBA was more traditional and had better-known teams.
Ⓑ The NBA had players with better skills.
Ⓒ The ABA was more colorful and exciting.
Ⓓ The ABA had more devoted fans.

LumosLearning.com

22. In the box below, write the letters of the two statements that tell how basketball became more popular in the 1980's.

Ⓐ TV stations began to promote basketball games.
Ⓑ Some great new players sparked excitement.
Ⓒ They started playing basketball in bigger arenas.
Ⓓ Schools began to require that students learn how to play basketball.
Ⓔ A rivalry developed between the Boston team and the Los Angeles team.

23. Part A.

What is the meaning of the word **marketing** as used in paragraph 8?

Ⓐ punishment for wrongdoing
Ⓑ promoting and selling something
Ⓒ getting rid of drugs
Ⓓ going to foreign countries

Part B.

Which detail from the story best supports your answer to Part A?

Ⓐ They were turned off by players' behavior off the court, such as drug use and other scandals.
Ⓑ Stern immediately instituted new tough-on-drugs policies.
Ⓒ NBA teams also play at least one game a year in a foreign country.
Ⓓ The NBA has grown five times as wealthy as it was when Stern first became Commissioner.

Unit 3

Read "The Song of Wandering Aengus" and answer the questions that follow

THE SONG OF WANDERING AENGUS
By W.B. Yeats

I went out to the hazel wood,
Because a fire was in my head,
And cut and peeled a hazel wand,
And hooked a berry to a thread;

And when white moths were on the wing,
And moth-like stars were flickering out,
I dropped the berry in a stream
And caught a little silver trout.

When I had laid it on the floor
I went to blow the fire a-flame,
But something rustled on the floor,
And someone called me by my name:

It had become a glimmering girl
With apple blossom in her hair,
Who called me by my name and ran
And faded through the brightening air.

Though I am old with wandering
Through hollow lands and hilly lands,
I will find out where she has gone,
And kiss her lips and take her hands;

And walk among long dappled grass,
And pluck till time and times are done
The silver apples of the moon,
The golden apples of the sun.

24. **What does the change in verb tense from the first stanza to the last indicate?**

    Ⓐ **The speaker is writing about a dream and is now awake.**
    Ⓑ **The speaker is looking forward to something that will happen.**
    Ⓒ **The speaker is thinking about something that happened in the past that affects the present and the future.**
    Ⓓ **The speaker wishes he could go back in time.**

25. What does the author explain in the final stanza?

Ⓐ He is older now and realizes he only imagined the girl.
Ⓑ He is an old man and is determined to find the girl.
Ⓒ He realizes he shall never find the girl.
Ⓓ He is tired of wandering around now looking for the girl.

26. According to the second stanza, what had become a **glittering girl**?

Ⓐ The silver trout
Ⓑ The moth
Ⓒ The magic wand
Ⓓ The red berry

27. What is the meaning of the title of the poem?

Ⓐ A girl named Aengus is wandering through the countryside.
Ⓑ Aengus is a synonym for wanderer.
Ⓒ Aengus will continue to wander until he finds the girl.
Ⓓ Aengus became lost on a trip and is looking for a way home.

28. Write a personal narrative about a time you wish you could go back in time and change an event.

Read "A Beginner's Guide to Effective Email" and answer the questions that follow.

A Beginner's Guide to Effective Email
by Kaitlin Duck Sherwood

INTRODUCTION

(1) I believe strongly in the value of email in both business and personal life. Email is cheaper and faster than a letter. It doesn't interrupt your day like a phone call. It's less hassle than using a fax machine. And it makes differences in location and time zone less important.

(2) Because of these advantages, email use is exploding. Overall, 82% of all American adults ages 18 and older say they use the internet or email at least occasionally, and 67% do so on a typical day (Pew, 2012).

(3) Sadly, in the twenty-plus years that I have been using email, I have seen a large number of people have problems because they did not understand how to adjust their communication styles to writing emails. I wrote this document to try to help people avoid those mistakes.

(4) This is not a document on the mechanics of sending email - which buttons to push or how to attach a photograph. I instead focus on the content of an email message: how to say what you need to say. I don't think of this as email etiquette (commonly called netiquette) because I don't think these guidelines merely show you how to be a nice person. These guidelines show you how to be more efficient, clear, and effective.

(5) This is not dogma. There will be people who disagree with me on specific points. But, if there was only one right answer, there wouldn't be a need to write this guide. Hopefully, this guide will make you examine your assumptions about email and thus help you write better emails.

WHAT MAKES EMAIL DIFFERENT?

(6) Electronic communication, because of its speed, is very different from paper-based communication. Because the turnaround time can be so fast, email is more conversational than traditional letters.

(7) In a paper document, it is absolutely essential to make everything complete-ly clear and unambiguous because your audience will not have the chance to ask a question. With email, your recipient can ask you to make things clearer immediately. Like speech, email tends to be a bit "sloppier" than communications on paper.

(8) This is not always bad. It makes little sense to slave over a message for hours, making sure that your spelling is faultless, your words eloquent, and your grammar perfect, if the point of the message is to tell your co-worker that you are ready to go to lunch.

(9) However, your correspondent also won't be able to see you face-to-face, and may make assumptions based on your name, address, and - above all - your ability to use words correctly. So you need to be aware of when you can be sloppy and when you have to be more careful.

(10) Email also does not convey emotions nearly as well as face-to-face or even telephone conversations. Your correspondent may have difficulty telling if you are seri-ous or kidding, happy or sad, frustrated or happy. It's especially hard to use sarcasm effectively in email.

(11) Another difference between email and older media is that what the sender sees when composing a message might not look like what the reader sees. Your vocal cords make sound waves that are perceived basically the same by both your ears as your audi-ence's. The paper that you write your love note on is the same paper that the object of your affection sees. But with email, the software and hardware that you use may be completely different from what your correspondent uses. How your message looks to you may be quite different from how it looks on someone else's screen.

(12) Thus your email compositions should be different from both your paper compositions and your speech.

     LumosLearning.com   ▼

29.   **Part A**

What is the theme of this passage?

Ⓐ Email is a different kind of communication that calls for different "rules" than phone conversations, notes, or letters.
Ⓑ Email and electronic media have made real communication more difficult.
Ⓒ Too many adults are using email to communicate when they should talk to people face-to-face.
Ⓓ Email programs should be made more alike so that people see the same thing no matter what computer they're on.

Part B.

Which detail from the passage best supports your answer to Part A?

Ⓐ How your message looks to you may be quite different from how it looks on someone else's screen.
Ⓑ Email also does not convey emotions nearly as well as face-to-face or even telephone conversations.
Ⓒ Thus your email compositions should be different from both your paper compositions and your speech.
Ⓓ Because the turnaround time can be so fast, email is more conversational than traditional letters.

30.   **Part A.**

What is the meaning of the word <u>**unambiguous**</u> as used in paragraph 7?

Ⓐ sloppy
Ⓑ clear
Ⓒ traditional
Ⓓ having perfect grammar

Part B.

Which detail from the story best supports your answer to Part A?

Ⓐ Like speech, email tends to be a bit "sloppier" than communications on paper.
Ⓑ because your audience will not have the chance to ask a question.
Ⓒ Email is more conversational than traditional letters.
Ⓓ making sure that your spelling is faultless, your words eloquent, and your grammar perfect

31. What is the importance of paragraph 10 in the passage? Write it in the box.

    Ⓐ to explain why phone conversations are better than email
    Ⓑ to describe the correct way to get an idea across in an email
    Ⓒ to tell about the author's experience in writing and receiving emails
    Ⓓ to explain that it is difficult to express emotions and humor in an email

© Lumos Information Services 2015   LumosLearning.com

Read "The Purpose of the Letter" and answer the questions that follow.

The Purpose of the Letter
by Mary Owens Crowther

(1)   A letter always has an object--otherwise why write it? But somehow, often a person will ramble all around what he wants to say and will end up using two pages for what he could have said in three lines. On the other hand, letters may be so brief as to produce an impression of discourtesy. It is a rare writer who can say all that need be said in one line and not seem rude. But it can be done.

(2)   The single purpose of a letter is to convey thought. That thought may have to do with facts, and the further purpose may be to have the thought produce action. Words as used in a letter are vehicles for thought, but there is a wide variation in the understanding of words. The average person's vocabulary is quite limited, and where an exactly phrased letter might completely convey an exact thought to a person of education, that same letter might be meaningless to a person who understands but few words. Therefore, it is a mistake in letter writing to use unusual words or to go much beyond ordinary vocabulary.

(3)   Some people feel that letters should be elegant. They think that that if someone expresses himself simply and clearly, it is because he is not very intelligent. There could be no greater mistake. The man who really knows the language will write simply. The man who does not know the language well pretends he does and ends up with a lot of flowery words that don't mean much.

(4)   Sometimes a person will be dreadfully afraid of making an error in public. He is afraid of getting hold of the wrong fork at dinner or of doing something else that is not supposed to be done. Such people take a very long time to write a simple letter.

(5)   But the person who understands proper behavior well observes the rules, not because they are rules, but because they are second nature to him. And he violates the rules if the occasion seems to call for it. It is quite the same with the letter writer.

(6)   One should know his ground well enough to do what one likes, bearing in mind that there is no reason for writing a letter unless the objective is clearly defined. Writing a letter is like shooting at a target. The target may be hit by accident, but it is more apt to be hit if careful aim has been taken.

32.   **Part A.**

What is the main idea of this passage?

Ⓐ A few people who write letters don't have a clue about how a letter should be written.
Ⓑ People who know how to behave well in public also know how to write good letters.
Ⓒ Letters should be brief and get directly to the point.
Ⓓ Letter-writers should use more interesting vocabulary to "spice up" their letters.

Part B.

Which detail from the passage best supports your answer to Part A?

Ⓐ It is a rare writer who can say all that need be said in one line and not seem rude. But it can be done.
Ⓑ But the person who understands proper behavior well observes the rules, not because they are rules, but because they are second nature to him.
Ⓒ Some people feel that letters should be elegant.
Ⓓ Therefore, it is a mistake in letter writing to use unusual words or to go much beyond ordinary vocabulary.

33.   **What is the author's opinion of the average person? Write your answer in the box.**

Ⓐ the average person likes getting a nice, long letter
Ⓑ the average person is not very intelligent
Ⓒ the average person is well-educated
Ⓓ the average person doesn't like to write letters

LumosLearning.com   ▼

34. **Part A.**

What is the meaning of the word <u>discourtesy</u> in paragraph 1?

Ⓐ briefness
Ⓑ unclearness
Ⓒ understanding courtesy
Ⓓ rudeness

Part B.

Which detail from the story best supports your answer to Part A?

Ⓐ Often a person will ramble all around what he wants to say.
Ⓑ The single purpose of a letter is to convey thought.
Ⓒ It is a rare writer who can say all that need be said in one line and not seem rude.
Ⓓ Letters may be so brief.

End of Summative Assessment (SA) - 2

Summative Assessment (SA) - 2

Answer Key

Question No.	Answer	Related Lumos Online Workbook	CCSS
Unit 1			
1 Part A	B	A matter of attitude	RL.7.4
1 Part B	C	A matter of attitude	RL.7.4
2	D	Prove it! (With evidence from the text); Use those clues - make an inference	RL.7.1
3	B	Prove it! (With evidence from the text); Use those clues - make an inference	RL.7.1
4	A	A matter of attitude	RL.7.4
5	A, C, D and B	One thing leads to another; When and where?; Who or what?	RL.7.3
6	C	What is it all about?	RL.7.2
7	*	Say what you mean	W.7.3
8 Part A	D	A matter of attitude	RL.7.4
8 Part B	C	Prove it! (With evidence from the text); Use those clues - make an inference	RL.7.1
9 Part A	C	One thing leads to another; When and where?; Who or what?	RL.7.3
9 Part B	A	Prove it! (With evidence from the text); Use those clues - make an inference	RL.7.1
10 Part A	B	How its made and what it means	RL.7.5
10 Part B	D	Prove it! (With evidence from the text); Use those clues - make an inference	RL.7.1
11	E, B, F, and C	What is it all about?; And the point of this is…?	RL.7.2
Unit 2			
12 Part A	D	Getting technical	RI.7.4
12 Part B	C	Prove it! (With evidence from the text)	RI.7.1
13	D, C, and A	How is it built? Analyzing structure	RI.7.5
14	A	Prove it! (With evidence from the text)	RI.7.1
15	B	Getting technical	RI.7.4

LumosLearning.com

▼

Question No.	Answer	Related Lumos Online Workbook	CCSS
16	A, D, and E	Equal? Alike? Different? Comparing authors	RI.7.9
	A, C and B		
17	D	Prove it! (With evidence from the text)	RI.7.1
18	*	Getting from here to there - transitions; A picture is worth a thousand words	W.7.2
19 Part A	A	Relationship between people and events	RI.7.3
19 Part B	C	Prove it! (With evidence from the text)	RI.7.1
20 Part A	D	Finding patterns - comparing and contrasting	RI.7.7
20 Part B	B and D	Prove it! (With evidence from the text)	RI.7.1
21	A and C	Prove it! (With evidence from the text)	RI.7.1
22	B and E	Get right to the point	RI.7.2
23 Part A	B	Getting technical	RI.7.4
23 Part B	D	Prove it! (With evidence from the text)	RI.7.1
Unit 3			
24	D	Prove it! (With evidence from the text)	RL.7.1
25	B	Prove it! (With evidence from the text)	RL.7.1
26	A	Prove it! (With evidence from the text)	RL.7.1
27	C	What is it all about?	RL.7.2
28	*	Say what you mean	W.7.3
29 Part A	A	Get right to the point	RI.7.2
29 Part B	C	Prove it! (With evidence from the text)	RI.7.1
30 Part A	B	Getting technical	RI 7.4
30 Part B	B	Prove it! (With evidence from the text)	RI.7.1
31	D	How is it built? Analyzing structure	RI.7.5
32 Part A	C	What is it all about?	RL 7.2
32 Part B	A	Prove it! (With evidence from the text)	RL 7.1
33	B	Finding patterns - comparing and contrasting	RL 7.7
34 Part A	D	A matter of attitude	RL 7.4
34 Part B	C	Prove it! (With evidence from the text)	RL 7.1

Summative Assessment (SA) - 2

Detailed Explanations

Question No.	Answer	Detailed Explanation
		Unit 1
1 Part A	B	Calamitous means disastrous which would also include catastrophic.
1 Part B	C	In the sentences following the word, the reader sees not only that the priesthood in Rome considered it dangerous, but that they protected it regularly.
2	D	Although twirling feet is mentioned, it is a stick and not twine that is used. Matches is the best answer because it is the method Claire mentions early in the passage.
3	B	Several times in the story, Uncle Paul explains to the **children** what happened when the fire went out.
4	A	Wane means dwindle and a synonym of dwindle is diminish or get smaller.
5	A, C, D and B	These are the events as they happened in the story.
6	C	Though A and B are true statements, they are not mentioned in both texts and they are not a major theme. The importance of protecting fire is the most important notion from both passages.
7		See Rubric Page No. 10 & 11
8 Part A	D	Gilded means painted gold
8 Part B	C	He looked like a gold top, because he was painted gold.
9 Part A	C	She thinks that she is too pretty for the top.
9 Part B	A	She would not even reply, showing she thought the top beneath her notice
10 Part A	B	This paragraph shows the the ball still thinks of herself as better than others.
10 Part B	D	"No one good enough to play with me" shows she is still very stuck-up.
11	E, B, F, and C	Summary: The top wants a playmate; the ball thinks she is too good for the top; the ball ends up in the trash can; the top goes back to the boy and the ball is thrown away.

LumosLearning.com ▼

Question No.	Answer	Detailed Explanation
		Unit 2
12 Part A	D	A quarrel is defined as an angry disagreement or altercation. Care must be taken to read the options carefully because option C describes an alteration (fixing clothing).
12 Part B	C	The fact that Jackson was in bed recovering from wounds indicates the disagreement he had was an angry one.
13	D, C, and A	This is the order the most important events occurred. Although B and E are actual events from the passage, they are not necessary to an understanding of Jackson.
14	A	As the name suggests, hickory is a strong wood that will bend but not break easily. The passage never indicates it is the strongest wood.
15	B	To trifle with something means to play with it or mess with it.
16	A, D, and E A, C and B	Analyzing both passages takes careful consideration. The details listed in these boxes most appropriately align with the correct passages. Option A is the only answer choice that is mentioned in both versions.
17	D	The qualities listed here best describe why he was a good scout.
18		See Rubric Page No. 10 & 11
19 Part A	A	He wanted to punish drug use and to promote basketball.
19 Part B	C	"tough on drugs" and "brilliant marketing" are the key words here
20 Part A	D	The passage traces the history of basketball; though it tells about David Stern, he is not the main focus.
20 Part B	B and D	Countries all over the world are playing it; that tells you it has grown to an international sport.
21	A and C	The passage states that the NBA was more traditional and the ABA more colorful.
22	B and E	The great new players and the team rivalry are mentioned as things that sparked interest.
23 Part A	B	Marketing means promoting and selling
23 Part B	D	The NBA becoming richer shows he was able to sell it better.
		Unit 3
24	D	In the beginning of the poem, the author is remembering. Once the verb changes, he also changes as well, now talking about how he wished he could change things and go back in time.

Question No.	Answer	Detailed Explanation
25	B	Although he is older now, the author is still determined to find the girl. These last two stanzas explain that desire.
26	A	The poem explicitly says it is the silver trout that became the glimmering girl.
27	C	Aengus is the speaker of the poem. He has been wandering looking for the "glimmering girl" and he will continue looking for her.
28		See Rubric Page No. 10 & 11
29 Part A	A	The theme is that email calls for different rules than other kinds of communication.
29 Part B	C	Choice C sums up the fact that it is different from other forms of communication.
30 Part A	B	Unambiguous means clear.
30 Part B	B	Saying you won't be able to ask a question means you need to be very clear the first time.
31	D	The author wants us to understand the limitations of email, particularly that it's difficult to convey emotion.
32 Part A	C	The author argues that letters should be brief and clear and make a point directly.
32 Part B	A	"It can be done" shows she is arguing for her readers to do it.
33	B	The author seems to think the average person is not very smart, because he does not understand advanced vocabulary, and does not know how to write a proper letter.
34 Part A	D	Discourtesy is rudeness.
34 Part B	C	The phrase "seem rude" tells you the meaning of discourtesy

              ▼

Practice Section

In this section, you will see additional passages and practice questions.

Practice: Literary Text

Read "The Two Travelers" and answer the questions that follow

THE TWO TRAVELERS
Retold by Maude Barrows Dutton

(1)   TWO Friends, Ganem and Salem, were journeying together, when they came to a broad stream at the foot of a hill. The woods were near at hand, and the shade was so welcome after the heat of the desert that they halted here to rest. After they had eaten and slept, they arose to go on, when they discovered near at hand a white stone, upon which was written in curious lettering this inscription:—

(2)   Travelers, we have prepared an excellent banquet for your refreshment; but you must be bold and deserve it before you can obtain it. What you are to do is this: throw yourselves bravely into the stream and swim to the other side. You will find there a lion carved from marble. This statue you must lift upon your shoulders and, with one run, carry to the top of yonder mountain, never heeding the thorns which prick your feet nor the wild beasts that may be lurking in the bushes to devour you. When once you have gained the top of the mountain, you will find yourselves in possession of great happiness.

(3)   Ganem was truly delighted when he read these words. "See, Salem," he cried, "here lies the road which will lead us to the end of all our travels and labor. Let us start at once, and see if what the stone says be true."

(4)   Salem, however, was of another mind. "Perhaps," he made answer, "this writing is but the jest of some idle beggar. Perhaps the current of the stream runs too swiftly for any man to swim it. Perhaps the lion is too heavy to carry, even if it be there. It is almost impossible that any one could reach the top of yonder mountain in one run. Take my word, it is not worth while to attempt any such mad venture. I for one will have no part in it."

(5)   Nevertheless, Ganem was not to be discouraged. "My mind is fully made up to try it," he replied, "and if you will not go with me, I must go alone." So the two friends embraced, and Salem rode off on his camel.

(6)   He was scarcely out of sight before Ganem had stripped off his clothes and thrown himself into the stream. He soon found that he was in the midst of a whirlpool, but he kept bravely on, and at last reached the other side in safety. When he had rested a few moments on the beach, he lifted the marble lion with one mighty effort, and with one run reached the top of the mountain. Here he saw to his great surprise that he was standing before the gates of a beautiful city. He was gazing at it in admiration, when strange roars came from the inside of the lion on his shoulder. The roaring grew louder and louder, until finally the turrets of the city were trembling and the mountain-sides reechoing with the tumult. Then Ganem saw to his astonishment that great crowds of people were pouring out of the city gates. They did not seem afraid of the noise, for they all wore smiling faces. As they came nearer, Ganem saw that they were led by a group of young noblemen, who held by the rein a prancing black charger. Slowly they advanced and knelt before Ganem, saying,—

(7)   "Brave stranger, we beseech thee to put on these regal robes which we are bringing, and, mounted upon this charger, ride back with thy subjects to the city."

(8)   Ganem, who could scarcely believe his ears, begged them to explain to him the meaning of these honors, and the noble youths replied,—

(9)   "Whenever our king dies, we place upon the stone by the river the inscription which you have read. Then we wait patiently until a traveler passes by who is brave enough to undertake the bold venture. Thus we are always assured that our king is a man who is fearless of heart and dauntless of purpose. We crown you to-day as King over our city."

1. **PART A**

In the box below write the letter of the characteristic that would accurately complete the Venn Diagram of Characteristics of Ganem and Salem from the story, "The Two Travelers."

Ⓐ **Friendly**
Ⓑ **Caring**
Ⓒ **Lazy**
Ⓓ **Hyper**

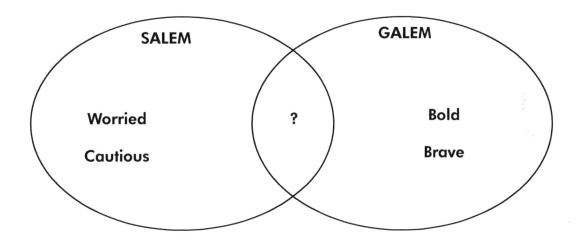

Part B

Write 2 paragraph numbers in the box below that support your answer in Part A.

2. **What is the theme of the story "The Two Travelers"?**

Ⓐ **Always take the advice good friends give you.**
Ⓑ **Don't be afraid to try things that seem impossible.**
Ⓒ **Never, never give up.**
Ⓓ **The ways of the world will fall away, but good friends always remain.**

3.   How is Salem's view of the situation different than Ganem's?

    Ⓐ Salem sees this as a scary situation he wants no part of doing.
    Ⓑ Ganem sees this as a complete waste of time.
    Ⓒ Salem sees this as a chance to meet new people and experience new things.
    Ⓓ Ganem sees this as an opportunity and an adventure.

4.   What is the meaning of the word **inscription** as it is used in paragraph 1 in the above passage?

    Ⓐ Identification
    Ⓑ Memorial
    Ⓒ Engraving
    Ⓓ Directory

LumosLearning.com

Read "Glimmerings" and answer the questions that follow.

Glimmerings
By Earnest Thompson Seton

(1)   Yan was much like other twelve-year-old boys in having a keen interest in Indians and in wildlife, but he differed from most in this, that he never got over it. Indeed, as he grew older, he found a yet keener pleasure in storing up the little bits of woodcraft and Indian lore that pleased him as a boy.

(2)   His father was in poor circumstances. He was an upright man of refined tastes, but indolent--a failure in business, easy with the world and stern with his family. He had never taken an interest in his son's wildwood pursuits; and when he got the idea that they might interfere with the boy's education, he forbade them altogether.

(3)   There was certainly no reason to accuse Yan of neglecting school. He was the head boy of his class, although there were many in it older than himself. He was fond of books in general, but those that dealt with Natural Science and Indian craft were very close to his heart.

(4)   Not that he had many--there were very few in those days, and the Public Library had but a poor representation of these. "Lloyd's Scandinavian Sports," "Gray's Botany" and one or two Fennimore Cooper novels, these were all, and Yan was devoted to them. He was a timid, obedient boy in most things, but the unwise command to give up what was his nature made him a disobedient boy. It turned a good boy into a bad one. He was too much in terror of his father to disobey openly, but he used to sneak away at all opportunities to the fields and woods, and at each new bird or plant he found he had an exquisite thrill of mingled pleasure and pain--the pain because he had no name for it or means of learning its nature.

(5)   The intense interest in animals was his master passion, and thanks to this, his course to and from school was a very crooked one, involving many crossings of the street, because thereby he could pass first a saloon in whose window was an advertisement that portrayed two terriers chasing a rat; next, directly opposite this, was a tobacco shop, in the window of which was a beautiful picture of an elephant, carrying tobacco. By going a little farther out of his way, there was a game store where he might see some ducks, and was sure, at least, of a stuffed deer's head. Beyond that was a furrier shop, with an astonishing stuffed bear. At yet another place on Jarvis Street was a cottage with a high veranda, under which, he was told, a chained bear had once been kept.

(6)   He never saw the bear. It had been gone for years, but he found pleasure in passing the place. At the corner of Pemberton and Grand streets, according to a schoolboy tradition, a skunk had been killed years ago and could still be smelled on damp nights. He always stopped, if passing near on a wet night, and sniffed and enjoyed that skunk smell. The fact that it ultimately turned out to be a leakage of sewer gas could never rob him of the pleasure he found in it.

(7)   Yan had no good excuse for these weaknesses, and he blushed for shame when his elder brother talked "common sense" to him about his follies. He only knew that such things fascinated him.

(8)   But the crowning glory was a taxidermist's shop kept on Main Street by a man named Sander. Yan spent many weeks gazing spellbound, with his nose flat against that window. It contained some fox and cat heads grinning ferociously, and about fifty birds beautifully displayed. Nature might have got some valuable hints in that window on showing plumage to the very best advantage. Each bird seemed more wonderful than the last.

(9)   There were perhaps fifty of them on view, and of these, twelve had labels, as they had formed part of an exhibit at the Annual County Fair. These labels were precious truths to him, and the birds were, with their names, deeply impressed on his memory and added to his wood lore. However, the labels were not always correct. For the alleged wood thrush was not a wood thrush at all, but turned out to be a hermit thrush. The last bird of the list was a long-tailed, brownish bird with white breast. The label was placed so that Yan could not read it from outside, and one of his daily occupations was to see if the label had been turned so that he could read it. But it never was, so he never learned the bird's name.

(10)   After passing this for a year or more, he formed a desperate plan. It was nothing less than to…go inside! It took him some months to screw up courage, for he was shy and timid, but oh, he was so hungry for it. Most likely if he had gone in openly and asked, he would have been allowed to see everything; but he did not dare. His home training was of the crushing kind. He picked on the most curious of the small birds in the window--a saw whet owl--then grit his teeth and walked in. How frightfully the cowbell on the door did clang! Then there was a still more appalling silence, then a step and the great man himself came.

(11)   "How--how--how much is that Owl?"

(12)   "Two dollars."

(13)   Yan's courage broke down now. He fled. If he had been told ten cents, it would have been utterly beyond reach. He scarcely heard what the man said. He hurried out with a vague feeling that he had been in heaven but was not good enough to stay there. He saw nothing more of the wonderful things around him.

5.   **Part A.**

Which phrase best describes the character of Yan?

Ⓐ lazy
Ⓑ bold
Ⓒ disobedient
Ⓓ eager to learn

Part B.

Which detail from the story provides the best evidence for the answer to Part A?

Ⓐ How frightfully the cowbell on the door did clang!
Ⓑ Yan spent many weeks gazing spellbound, with his nose flat against that window.
Ⓒ He blushed for shame when his elder brother talked "common sense" to him about his follies.
Ⓓ It took him some months to screw up courage

6.   **Part A**

What is the theme of this passage?

Ⓐ Schooling is more important than other means of education.
Ⓑ Taxidermists should make sure they have the correct information when they label animals.
Ⓒ Children should be allowed to pursue their natural interests.
Ⓓ Nature study is a rewarding occupation.

Part B.

Which detail from the passage best supports your answer to Part A?

Ⓐ He was a timid, obedient boy in most things, but the unwise command to give up what was his nature made him a disobedient boy.
Ⓑ For the alleged wood thrush was not a wood thrush at all, but turned out to be a hermit thrush.
Ⓒ There was certainly no reason to accuse Yan of neglecting school.
Ⓓ at each new bird or plant he found he had an exquisite thrill of mingled pleasure and pain--the pain because he had no name for it or means of learning its nature.

7.   **What is the importance of paragraph 10 in the passage? Write your answer in the box.**

Ⓐ It shows how timid Yan was, yet how eager he was to learn.
Ⓑ It explains why the taxidermist did not want to let Yan in.
Ⓒ It describes the home life of Yan and his brothers.
Ⓓ It tells about the various kinds of birds that Yan liked

```
┌──────────────────────────────┐
│                              │
│                              │
│                              │
│                              │
└──────────────────────────────┘
```

8   **Part A.**

What is the meaning of the word <u>indolent</u> in paragraph 2?

Ⓐ eager to learn
Ⓑ easily pleased
Ⓒ lazy
Ⓓ timid

Part B.

Which detail best supports your answer to Part A?

Ⓐ His father was in poor circumstances.
Ⓑ He was a failure in business, easy with the world and stern with his family. He had never taken an interest in his son's wildwood pursuits
Ⓒ His home training was of the crushing kind.
Ⓓ He was the head boy of his class, although there were many in it older than himself.

Read "The Story of Doctor Doolittle" and answer the questions that follow.

The Story of Doctor Doolittle
By Hugh Lofting

The Second Chapter: Animal Language

(1)   It happened one day that the Doctor was sitting in his kitchen talking with the Catfood-Man who had come to see him with a stomach-ache.

(2)   "Why don't you give up being a people's doctor, and be an animal-doctor?" asked the Catfood-Man.

(3)   The parrot, Polynesia, was sitting in the window looking out at the rain and singing a sailor-song to herself. She stopped singing and started to listen.

(4)   "You see, Doctor," the Catfood-Man went on, "you know all about animals--much more than what these here vets do. That book you wrote--about cats, why, it's wonderful! I can't read or write myself, or maybe I'd write some books. But my wife, Theodosia, she's a scholar, she is. And she read your book to me. Well, it's wonderful--that's all can be said--wonderful. You might have been a cat yourself. You know the way they think. And listen: you can make a lot of money doctoring animals. Do you know that? You see, I'd send all the old women who had sick cats or dogs to you. And if they didn't get sick fast enough, I could put something in the meat I sell 'em to make 'em sick, see?"

(5)   "Oh, no," said the Doctor quickly. "You mustn't do that. That wouldn't be right."

(6)   "Oh, I didn't mean real sick," answered the Catfood-Man. "Just a little something to make them droopy-like was what I had reference to. But as you say, maybe it ain't quite fair on the animals. But they'll get sick anyway, because the old women always give 'em too much to eat. And look, all the farmers 'round about who had lame horses and weak lambs--they'd come. Be an animal-doctor."

(7)   When the Catfood Man had gone the parrot flew off the window on to the Doctor's table and said, "That man's got sense. That's what you ought to do. Be an animal-doctor. Give the silly people up--if they haven't brains enough to see you're the best doctor in the world. Take care of animals instead—they'll soon find it out. Be an animal-doctor."

(8)   "Oh, there are plenty of animal-doctors," said John Doolittle, putting the flower-pots outside on the window-sill to get the rain.

(9) "Yes, there ARE plenty," said Polynesia. "But none of them are any good at all. Now listen, Doctor, and I'll tell you something. Did you know that animals can talk?"

(10) "I knew that parrots can talk," said the Doctor.

(11) "Oh, we parrots can talk in two languages--people's language and bird-language," said Polynesia proudly. "If I say, 'Polly wants a cracker,' you understand me. But hear this: Ka-ka oi-ee, fee-fee?"

(12) "Good Gracious!" cried the Doctor. "What does that mean?"

(13) "That means, 'Is the porridge hot yet?'--in bird-language."

(14) "My! You don't say so!" said the Doctor. "You never talked that way to me before."

(15) "What would have been the good?" said Polynesia, dusting some cracker-crumbs off her left wing. "You wouldn't have understood me if I had."

(16) "Tell me some more," said the Doctor, all excited; and he rushed over to the dresser-drawer and came back with the butcher's book and a pencil. "Now don't go too fast--and I'll write it down. This is interesting--very interesting--something quite new. Give me "the Birds' A.B.C." first--slowly now."

(17) So that was the way the Doctor came to know that animals had a language of their own and could talk to one another. And all that afternoon, while it was raining, Polynesia sat on the kitchen table giving him bird words to put down in the book.

(18) At tea-time, when the dog, Jip, came in, the parrot said to the Doctor, "See, he's talking to you."

(19) "Looks to me as though he were scratching his ear," said the Doctor.

(20) "But animals don't always speak with their mouths," said the parrot in a high voice, raising her eyebrows. "They talk with their ears, with their feet, with their tails--with everything. Sometimes they don't want to make a noise. Do you see now the way he's twitching up one side of his nose?"

(21) "What's that mean?" asked the Doctor.

(22) "That means, 'Can't you see that it has stopped raining?'" Polynesia answered. "He is asking you a question. Dogs nearly always use their noses for asking questions."

LumosLearning.com

(23)   After a while, with the parrot's help, the Doctor got to learn the language of the animals so well that he could talk to them himself and understand everything they said. Then relinquished the title of a people- doctor altogether.

(24)   As soon as the Catfood Man had told everyone that John Doolittle was going to become an animal-doctor, old ladies began to bring him their pet pugs and poodles who had eaten too much cake; and farmers came many miles to show him sick cows and sheep.

9.   **Part A.**

      What is the theme of this passage?

      Ⓐ **People don't appreciate doctors, but animals do.**
      Ⓑ **You can learn something from animals' sounds and behaviors if you pay attention to them.**
      Ⓒ **Parrots can speak in two different languages.**
      Ⓓ **Veterinarians make a lot of money, because animals are always getting sick.**

      Part B.

      Which detail from the passage best supports your answer to Part A?

      Ⓐ **Farmers came many miles to show him sick cows and sheep.**
      Ⓑ **Oh, we parrots can talk in two languages--people's language and bird-language.**
      Ⓒ **Give the silly people up--if they haven't brains enough to see you're the best doctor in the world.**
      Ⓓ **They talk with their ears, with their feet, with their tails--with everything.**

10.   **What is the meaning of the word <u>relinquished</u> as used in paragraph 23? Circle your answer.**

      Ⓐ **gave up**
      Ⓑ **defended**
      Ⓒ **forgot**
      Ⓓ **held on to**

Practice: Informational Text

Read "Time Travel" and answer the questions that follow

Time Travel
Author Unknown

(1)   In the nineteenth century, time travel was the stuff of science fiction. No one imagined it might someday be a reality. In 1895, H.G. Wells published a novel called The Time Machine. In this work of fiction the protagonist, who is never named, travels hundreds of thousands of years into the future.

(2)   While Wells' novel was not the first work of fiction to cover time travel, it was the first to spend time trying to explain the science behind this seemingly impossible feat. Wells theorized that when people viewed objects in three dimensions, there also existed a fourth dimension, time. Time, thought Wells, is invisible, but we can still move through it.

(3)   In chapter one, the Time Traveler elaborates on the fourth dimension, "'Now, it is very remarkable that this is so extensively overlooked,' continued the Time Traveler, with a slight accession of cheerfulness. 'Really this is what is meant by the Fourth Dimension, though some people who talk about the Fourth Dimension do not know they mean it. It is only another way of looking at Time. There is no difference between time and any of the three dimensions of space except that our consciousness moves along it. But some foolish people have got hold of the wrong side of that idea." (Wells, p. 5)

(4)   In other words, proposed Wells, we travel to the left, to the right, up, and down, using our bodies. But we travel through time using our minds. We can remember yesterday. We can remember last year. When we wake up in the morning, we know it is not the same day as it was yesterday. Therefore, according to Wells, we travel with our consciousness. Someone confined to his or her bed might not move at all in the three visible dimensions, but he or she can continue to move through the fourth. On the other hand, someone confined to a bed who was unconscious might wake up and ask, "What day is it?" The loss of consciousness would have stopped that person from traveling in the fourth dimension, time.

(5)   Wells' ideas made for very detailed fiction. But maybe he was on to something! In 1905, Albert Einstein published his Theory of Special Relativity. Einstein proposed that there were four dimensions, and those dimensions included, up and down, left and right, forward and backward, and one dimension of time. He linked space and time together. He proposed that if one traveled through space, on a straight line, at a high enough speed, one's observations about the world around him or her would be different from those traveling at a slower speed. In a nutshell, Einstein believed that if people could travel at the speed of light, they would be freed from the constraints of time, and free to travel to the future or to the past.

(6)   Over one hundred years later, the greatest scientists on the planet are still grappling with Einstein's proposal. Stephen Hawking, a well-known physicist, is convinced that time travel might be possible, but only to travel into the future. He believes that time, as a fourth dimension, must have wrinkles or tunnels, and that it is porous. Hawking believes if someone had a rocket that was fast enough, one that could travel at the speed of light, he or she could travel through one of those tunnels and skip ahead in time. He hasn't completely abandoned the idea of traveling to the past, though. He's just waiting for evidence that it is possible. In 2012, Hawking said, "I gave a party for time-travelers, but I didn't send out the invitations until after the party. I sat there a long time, but no one came."

11.   **You just read a passage which contains three different points of view of time: Wells', Einstein's, and Hawking's. Each individual had his own theory of how time functions as a dimension. Several of the ideas are listed below. From the list, place the correct descriptive phrase into correct box. Some phrases may be used in more than one box and some phrases may not be used at all.**

Possible descriptions

Ⓐ **believes time is considered a 4th dimension**
Ⓑ **believes it is possible to explore when traveling at the speed of light**
Ⓒ **believes it is possible to travel back and forth through time**
Ⓓ **believes it is possible to travel forwards only**
Ⓔ **believes times has wrinkles**

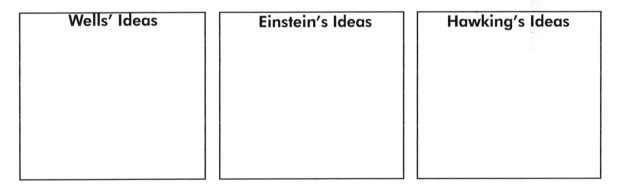

Wells' Ideas	Einstein's Ideas	Hawking's Ideas

12.   **Select the phrase that best completes the following sentence.**

When comparing the information presented in "Time Travel" and "Double Davids", it is clear the two different authors,

Ⓐ **believe science is the best way to explain time travel**
Ⓑ **do not believe time travel is possible**
Ⓒ **use a variety of techniques to explain time travel**
Ⓓ **have the exact same viewpoint on time travel**

Read "Building a Canoe" and answer the questions that follow

BUILDING A CANOE
By Lawton B. Evans

(1)   THE birch bark canoe was the most beautiful and ingenious of all the Indians' inventions. It was so broad that it could float in shallow streams, so strong that it could shoot dangerous rapids, and so light that one man could easily carry it on his back.

(2)   To make such a boat the Indians picked out a tall tree, with thick bark and with as few branches as possible. This they would cut down, care being taken to prevent it falling against other trees, thereby hurting the bark. The bark was then split along the length of the tree, and carefully peeled off in pieces the length and breadth of the canoe. They were very particular not to have any holes in the bark, which, during the season when the sap was in the tree, was firm and fine.

(3)   The bark was then spread on the ground in a smooth place, the inside downwards, and, in order to stretch it better, logs of wood or stones were placed on it. Then the edges of the bark were gently bent upwards to form the sides of the boat. Some sticks were fixed into the ground at a distance of three or four feet from each other, forming the curved line which the sides of the boat were intended to make. The bark was bent to the form which the boat was to have, being held firmly in position by the sticks thus driven into the ground.

(4)   The ribs of the boat were made of tough hickory, cut into long, flat pieces, and bent to the shape of the boat, the wider ones in the middle, and the narrower ones towards the ends. When thus bent and tied in position, the ribs were placed upon the bark about ten inches apart.

(5)   The upper edge of each side of the boat was made of two thin poles, the boat's length, and put close together with flat edges to hold the bark between. These long poles, firmly attached to the ribs, determined the shape of the boat. The edge of the bark was now inserted between the poles on each side, and was sewed to the poles by means of mouse-wood, bark, or roots.

(6)   The poles were now sewed together at the end, and the bark was made water tight where it was joined by pounded bark of the red elm. Bands were placed across the top of the ribs of the boat to prevent spreading or crushing in, and boards were laid across the bottom to step on. The boat was then ready for use.

(7)   This was a frail structure, and had to be treated very tenderly. The sides were easily torn open by rocks and hidden branches of trees, and, therefore, the Indian was always on the lookout for danger. The bottom could be easily crushed through; hence the Indian went barefoot, and entered the canoe very gingerly.

                   LumosLearning.com   ◄

(8)   But with such a canoe three or four persons could easily float, and in some of the war canoes even a dozen Indians could find space. With long paddles and strong arms, the Indians forced their craft over the lakes and along the rivers with great ease and speed. It was strong enough to hold a heavy load, so long as it did not strike a rock or hidden tree. Such a boat could shoot down a dangerous rapid, if it was directed by skillful hands. When the Indians wished to move from one lake to another, they lifted the canoe out the water, strapped it across the back of one man, who took it over the trail across country from one body of water to another.

13.   **Create a summary of the passage "How to Build a Canoe" by writing the letters of three sentences into the summary boxes, in the correct order. The sentences should describe important events or ideas from the story.**

Ⓐ **But with such a canoe three or four persons could easily float, and in some of the war canoes even a dozen Indians could find space.**

Ⓑ **To make such a boat the Indians picked out a tall tree, with thick bark and with as few branches as possible.**

Ⓒ **This was a frail structure, and had to be treated very tenderly.**

Ⓓ **The bottom could be easily crushed through; hence the Indian went bare foot, and entered the canoe very gingerly.**

Ⓔ **The birch bark canoe was the most beautiful and ingenious of all the Indians' inventions.**

Ⓕ **The bark was bent to the form which the boat was to have, being held firmly in position by the sticks thus driven into the ground.**

Summary 1

Summary 2

Summary 3

14. **PART A**

What is a synonym for the word <u>frail</u> as it is used in paragraph 7 of the above passage?

Ⓐ Delicate
Ⓑ Strong
Ⓒ Bare
Ⓓ Contained

PART B

What evidence from the text supports your answer in PART A?

Ⓐ Some sticks were fixed into the ground at a distance of three or four feet from each other, forming the curved line which the sides of the boat were intended to make.
Ⓑ This was a frail structure, and had to be treated very tenderly.
Ⓒ But with such a canoe three or four persons could easily float, and in some of the war canoes even a dozen Indians could find space.
Ⓓ With long paddles and strong arms, the Indians forced their craft over the lakes and along the rivers with great ease and speed.

15. What is the overall purpose of the final paragraph of "Building a Canoe"?

Ⓐ It explains how the poles are attached together and how they function.
Ⓑ It explains the process used to determine which trees are the best to use.
Ⓒ It explains how the ribs of the boat are made and how they function.
Ⓓ It explains how the delicate boat can be used once it is complete.

16. How does the overall structure of the passage help the reader understand the unique process utilized to build a canoe?

Ⓐ The passage is broken into sections of key information.
Ⓑ The passage is broken into sections that includes different ways Indians build canoes
Ⓒ The passage is broken into paragraphs where each details specific steps.
Ⓓ The passage is broken into paragraphs of chronological order.

17. Select two sentences from the text above that support the author's primary claim in paragraph 1 which states, "THE birch bark canoe was the most beautiful and ingenious of all the Indians' inventions." Write your sentences, and their paragraph number into the box below.

Read "Adelie Penguins" and answer the questions that follow.

Adelie Penguins
by George Murray Levick

(1) The penguins of the Antarctic regions very rightly have been called the true inhabitants of that country. The species is very old. Fossil remains of their ancestors having been found which showed that they have lived there for a long time. The penguin has adapted itself to the sea, like the fishes. This skill in the water has been gained at the loss of its power of flight, but this is not terribly important.

(2) In few other regions could such an animal as the penguin raise its young. When on land its short legs make it hard to get around, and as it cannot fly, it would become an easy prey to other animals. Here, however, since there are no bears or foxes here, once ashore the penguin is safe.

(3) The reason for this is that there is no food on the land. Many ages ago, a different state of things existed: there were tropical forests here and at one time, the seals ran about on shore like dogs. As conditions changed, they had to take to the sea for food. Then over time, their four legs became wide paddles or "flippers," as the penguins' wings have done, so that at length they became true inhabitants of the sea.

(4) If the seals (the Adelies' worst enemy) came back on the land again, there would be an end to all the southern penguin rookeries. As these, however, are inhabited only during four and a half months of the year, the advantage to the seals in growing legs again would not be great enough to influence evolution in that direction. At the same time, I wonder very much that the seals, who can squirm along at a fair pace on land, have not crawled up the few yards of ice between the water and some of the rookeries. Even if they could not catch the old birds, they could feast on the chicks when they are hatched. Fortunately however they never do this.

(5) When seen for the first time, the Adelie penguin gives you the impression of a very smart little man in an evening dress suit, so clean-looking is he, with his shimmering white front and black back and shoulders. He stands about two feet five inches in height, walking very upright on his little legs.

(6) He is confident as he approaches you over the snow, curiosity in his every movement. When within a yard or two of you, as you stand watching him, he stops. Poking his head forward with little jerky movements, first to one side, then to the other, he uses his right and left eye alternately during his inspection. He seems to prefer using one eye at a time when viewing any near object, but when looking far ahead, or walking along, he looks straight ahead of him, using both eyes. He does this, too, when his anger is aroused, holding his head very high, and appearing to squint at you along his beak.

         LumosLearning.com

(7)   After a careful inspection, he may suddenly lose all interest in you, and ruffling up his feathers sink into a doze. Stand still for a minute till he has settled himself to sleep, then make sound enough to wake him without startling him, and he opens his eyes, stretching himself, yawns, then finally walks off, caring no more about you.

18.   **Part A.**

   Which of the following best describes an Adelie penguin?

   Ⓐ a small black and white penguin
   Ⓑ a large penguin that used to live in the sea
   Ⓒ a seal that used to live on land like a dog
   Ⓓ a shy penguin that scientists have not been able to approach

   Part B.

   Which detail from the story best supports your answer to part A?

   Ⓐ They ran about on shore like dogs. As conditions changed, they had to take to the sea for food.
   Ⓑ They could feast on the chicks when they are hatched.
   Ⓒ With his shimmering white front and black back and shoulders, he stands about two feet five inches in height.
   Ⓓ He opens his eyes, stretching himself, yawns, then finally walks off, caring no more about you.

19.   **Part A.**

   What is the main idea of this passage?

   Ⓐ The seal is the Adelie penguin's worst enemy.
   Ⓑ Many penguin chicks are eaten by seals every year.
   Ⓒ The Adelie penguin is well adapted to its environment.
   Ⓓ Antarctica is not a good environment for most animals.

   Part B

   Which detail from the story best supports your answer to Part A?

   Ⓐ If the seals (the Adelies' worst enemy) came back on the land again, there would be an end to all the southern penguin rookeries.
   Ⓑ They could feast on the chicks when they are hatched.
   Ⓒ The penguin has adapted itself to the sea, like the fishes.
   Ⓓ The reason for this is that there is no food on the land.

20. Why does the author give so much information about seals in a passage about penguins?

Ⓐ Seals have been important in the development of the penguin.
Ⓑ Seals are the penguins' worst enemy.
Ⓒ Seals are more interesting creatures than penguins.
Ⓓ Seals help protect penguins' chicks.

21. What is the importance of paragraph 6 in the passage?

Ⓐ It explains why humans should leave penguins alone.
Ⓑ It tells how penguins get their food.
Ⓒ It explains why penguins live in Antarctica.
Ⓓ It describes how the penguin acts when it meets a human.

22. Part A

What is the meaning of the word <u>rookeries</u> as used in paragraph 4?

Ⓐ places where penguins lay eggs and raise their young
Ⓑ places where penguins hunt for food
Ⓒ places where penguins hide from seals
Ⓓ young penguins

Part B

Which detail from the passage best supports your answer to Part A?

Ⓐ He does this, too, when his anger is aroused, holding his head very high.
Ⓑ chicks when they are hatched
Ⓒ That at length they became true inhabitants of the sea.
Ⓓ If the seals came back on the land again, there would be an end to all the southern penguin rookeries.

End of Practice Section

LumosLearning.com ◀

Practice Section

Answer Key

Question No.	Answer	Related Lumos Online Workbook	CCSS
		Literary Practice	
1 Part A	A	One thing leads to another; When and where?	RL.7.3
1 Part B	1 and 5	One thing leads to another; When and where?	RL.7.3
2	B	What is it all about?; And the point of this is...?	RL.7.2
3	D	What a character!	RL.7.6
4	C	A matter of attitude	RL.7.4
5 Part A	D	One thing leads to another; When and where?; Who or what?	RL.7.3
5 Part B	B	Prove it! (With evidence from the text); Use those clues - make an inference	RL.7.1
6 Part A	C	What is it all about?; And the point of this is...?	RL.7.2
6 Part B	A	Prove it! (With evidence from the text); Use those clues - make an inference	RL 7.1
7	A	How its made and what it means	RL.7.5
8 Part A	C	A matter of attitude	RL.7.4
8 Part B	B	Prove it! (With evidence from the text); Use those clues - make an inference	RL.7.1
9 Part A	B	Get right to the point	RI.7.2
9 Part B	D	Prove it! (With evidence from the text)	RI 7.1
10	A	Getting technical	RI.7.4
		Informational Practice	
11	Wells: A and C Einstein: A, B, and C Hawking: A, D, and E	Whats the authors angle?	RI.7.6
12	C	Equal? Alike? Different? Comparing authors	RI.7.9
13	E, B, and A	Get right to the point	RI.7.2
14 Part A	A	Figuring it out with context clues	L.7.4

Question No.	Answer	Related Lumos Online Workbook	CCSS
14 Part B	B	Figuring it out with context clues	L.7.4
15	D	Get right to the point	RI.7.2
16	C	How is it built? Analyzing structure	RI.7.5
17	Paragraphs 1 and 8	Whats the authors point?	RI.7.8
18 Part A	A	Relationship between people and events	RI.7.3
18 Part B	C	Prove it! (With evidence from the text)	RI.7.1
19 Part A	C	Get right to the point	RI.7.2
19 Part B	C	Prove it! (With evidence from the text)	RI 7.1
20	B	Finding patterns - comparing and contrasting	RI.7.7
21	D	How is it built? Analyzing structure	RI.7.5
22 Part A	A	Getting technical	RI.7.4
22 Part B	B	Prove it! (With evidence from the text)	RI.7.1

LumosLearning.com

Practice Section

Detailed Explanations

Question No.	Answer	Detailed Explanation
		Literary Practice
1 Part A	A	This Venn Diagram is looking for the character trait the two men have in common. According to the text, they are both friendly.
1 Part B	1 and 5	These two paragraphs discuss the two men as friends and show them embracing.
2	B	Although the story mentions two friends, their friendship is not the central theme of the story, and the author does not focus on Salem not giving up. Instead, he focuses on the reward Salem receives because he was not afraid to try what seemed impossible.
3	D	Salem is not afraid of the situation before them, but he is very cautious and wary. On the other hand, Ganem sees this as a very good opportunity and is ready for the adventure.
4	C	An inscription is an engraving or carving of importance.
5 Part A	D	Much of the story describes how eager Yan is to learn about animals.
5 Part B	B	Spending many hours gazing through the window of the taxidermist shows that he is very eager to learn about the animals.
6 Part A	C	The passage shows the sad consequences for Yan because he is not allowed to follow his natural interests. He has to hide and sneak around and is afraid to even talk to the taxidermist.
6 Part B	A	It was unwise to forbid him to study nature, as the result was his becoming disobedient.
7	A	It shows how eager he was to see everything, yet he was so timid that he was afraid to ask.
8 Part A	C	Indolent means lazy.
8 Part B	B	He failed at business (possibly due to laziness), and he doesn't put any effort into understanding Yan
9 Part A	B	The theme is that you can learn things from watching and listening to animals.

Question No.	Answer	Detailed Explanation
9 Part B	D	Describing the different ways they communicate shows that you can learn something if you pay attention.
10	A	To relinquish means to give up.
Informational Practice		
11	Wells: A and C Einstein: A, B, and C Hawking: A, D, and E	The text offers the various viewpoints of the characters when it comes to the theories of time.
12	C	Although one passage is a fiction piece, and the other is informational both authors use a variety of techniques to explain time travel: science, fiction, movies, and literature.
13	E, B, and A	Although each of the choices was a direct quote, the three correct answers were the most important ideas. They are listed in the correct order.
14 Part A	A	The definition of frail is weak or easily broken; therefore, an appropriate synonym is delicate.
14 Part B	B	The fact that the canoe had to be treated tenderly is an example of how delicate the canoe was.
15	D	Each option offers a key idea of a specific paragraph, but only option D explains the key purpose of the final section.
16	C	Each section is a paragraph that functions as a step by step guide to building a canoe.
17	Paragraphs 1 and 8	Answers may vary but should include information from paragraphs 1 and 8 as primary claims of support.
18 Part A	A	It is described as being black and white, and small.
18 Part B	C	Two feet 5 inches is very small.
19 Part A	C	The passage talks about how the penguin can survive in this environment.
19 Part B	C	'has adapted itself to the sea' tells one way that it has adapted
20	B	Seals are mentioned because they are the penguin's main predator.
21	D	This paragraph helps us "see" what the penguin would act like if we could get close to him.
22 Part A	A	Rookeries are where they lay their eggs and raise their chicks.
22 Part B	B	The word "chicks" tells you what is in a rookery.

    LumosLearning.com

Notes

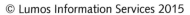

Lumos StepUp™ is an educational App that helps students learn and master grade-level skills in Math and English Language Arts.

The list of features includes:

- Learn Anywhere, Anytime!

- Grades 3-8 Mathematics and English Language Arts

- Get instant access to the Common Core State Standards

- One full-length sample practice test in all Grades and Subjects

- Full-length Practice Tests, Partial Tests and Standards-based Tests

- 2 Test Modes: Normal mode and Learning mode

- Learning Mode gives the user a step-by-step explanation if the answer is wrong

- Access to Online Workbooks

- Provides ability to directly scan QR Codes

- And it's completely FREE!

http://lumoslearning.com/a/stepup-app

Lumoslearning

About Online Workbooks

♦ When you buy this book, 1 year access to online workbooks included

♦ Access them anytime from a computer with an internet connection

♦ Adheres to the New Common Core State Standards

♦ Includes progress reports

♦ Instant feedback and self-paced

♦ Ability to review incorrect answers

♦ Parents and Teachers can assist in student's learning by reviewing their areas of difficulty

Course Name: Grade 4 Math Prep

Lesson Name:	Correct	Total	% Score	Incorrect
Introduction				
Diagnostic Test		3	0%	3
Number and Numerical Operations				
Workbook - Number Sense	2	10	20%	8
Workbook - Numerical Operations	2	25	8%	23
Workbook - Estimation	1	3	33%	2
Geometry and measurement				
Workbook - Geometric Properties		6	0%	6
Workbook - Transforming Shapes				
Workbook - Coordinate Geometry	1	3	33%	2
Workbook - Units of Measurement				
Workbook - Measuring Geometric Objects	3	10	30%	7
Patterns and algebra				
Workbook - Patterns	7	10	70%	3
Workbook - Functions and relationships				

LESSON NAME: Workbook - Geometric Properties
Elapsed Time: 01:19

Question No. 2
What type of motion is being modeled here?

Select right answer
- ◯ a translation
- ◯ a rotation 90° clockwise
- ◉ a rotation 90° counter-clockwise
- ◯ a reflection

[Previous question] [Next question]

Report Name: Missed Questions

Student Name: Lisa Colbright
Cours Name: Grade 4 Math Prep
Lesson Name: Diagnostic Test

The faces on a number cube are labeled with the numbers 1 through 6. What is the probability of rolling a number greater than 4?

Answer Explanation

(C) On a standard number cube, there are six possible outcomes. Of those outcomes, 2 of them are greater than 4. Thus, the probability of rolling a number greater than 4 is "2 out of 6" or 2/6.

A)		1/6
B)		1/3
C)	Correct Answer	2/6
D)		3/6

7
Grade

Lumos Learning
Developed By Expert Teachers

Common Core Assessments and Online Workbooks

PARCC 2016
Practice Tests
MATHEMATICS

☆ **2** Summative Assessments

★ Additional Questions by Type

☆ Includes access to the Mobile Apps

★ Answer Key and Detailed Explanations

PLUS ## Online Workbooks
With Hundreds of Practice Questions

Adheres to the Common Core State Standards
www.LumosLearning.com

Available
- **At Leading book stores**
- **Online www.LumosLearning.com**

Made in the USA
Middletown, DE
28 March 2016